PEL

A GUIDE TO

Tyrrell Burgess was born ... ...
and junior schools in Romford, Essex, and Tumble, Car-
marthenshire, where he was evacuated during the war. He
passed the 'scholarship' (as it was then called) – in Welsh –
to the Gwendraeth Valley Secondary School and went later
to the Royal Liberty School, Romford. He took an open
exhibition in history at Keble College, Oxford. On leaving
university he taught in several kinds of school, state and
independent, and then joined *The Times Educational Supplement*. He has been news editor of that journal, the first director
of the Advisory Centre for Education, assistant editor of *New
Society* and a Research Fellow in the Higher Education
Research Unit at the London School of Economics. He is
now Director of the Centre for Institutional Studies at the
North East London Polytechnic.

His books include *Inside Comprehensive Schools*, written for
the Department of Education and Science, and *Policy and
Practice: The Colleges of Advanced Technology* (written with
John Pratt), published by Allen Lane The Penguin Press. He
edited the Penguin Education Special *Dear Lord James: A
Critique of Teacher Education*. In 1964 he was Labour candi-
date for Croydon South, and he was a contributor to the
Penguin Special *Matters of Principle: Labour's Last Chance*.

TYRRELL BURGESS

A Guide to English Schools

Third Edition

PENGUIN BOOKS

Penguin Books Ltd, Harmondsworth, Middlesex, England
Penguin Books Inc., 7110 Ambassador Road, Baltimore, Maryland 21207, U.S.A.
Penguin Books Australia Ltd, Ringwood, Victoria, Australia

—

First published 1964
Reprinted 1966, 1967
Second edition 1969
Reprinted 1970
Third edition 1972

—

Copyright © Tyrrell Burgess, 1964, 1969, 1972

—

Made and printed in Great Britain
by Hazell Watson & Viney Ltd,
Aylesbury, Bucks
Set in Monotype Times

This book is sold subject to the condition
that it shall not, by way of trade or otherwise,
be lent, re-sold, hired out, or otherwise circulated
without the publisher's prior consent in any form of
binding or cover other than that in which it is
published and without a similar condition
including this condition being imposed
on the subsequent purchaser

For my parents

Contents

PREFACE	11
1 PEOPLE AND EDUCATION	15
2 THE LAW: THE EDUCATION ACT, 1944	17
WHAT THERE WAS BEFORE	18
Secondary Education	18
Elementary Education	19
WHAT THE ACT DID	20
3 ADMINISTERING EDUCATION	24
THE DEPARTMENT OF EDUCATION AND SCIENCE	24
Parliament	24
The Secretary of State	25
The Secretary of State's Functions	28
The Secretary of State's Day	30
Junior Ministers	30
Civil Servants	31
Policy and Practice	35
What the Department does	36
What the Department does not do	41
Consultation and Advice	42
LOCAL EDUCATION AUTHORITIES	51
Duties and Powers	53
Shapes and Sizes	55
Education Committees	56
THE AUTHORITIES – AND PARENTS	58
The Law	59
The Courts	60
The Secretary of State	62
The Local Authority	62
The School	63

CONTENTS

4 THE SCHOOLS	65
(i) SCHOOL ORGANIZATION	66
School 'Houses'	67
Prefects	68
Teachers	68
Teachers' Quota Scheme	70
Teachers' Salaries	70
Hierarchy and Freedom	72
(ii) KINDS OF SCHOOLS	73
STATE SCHOOLS	73
County and Voluntary Schools	74
Religious Instruction	76
Managers and Governors	77
Nursery Schools	80
Primary Schools	83
Infant Schools	84
Junior Schools	85
Middle Schools	85
All-Age Schools	86
Secondary Schools	86
Reorganization	86
Secondary Modern Schools	92
Grammar Schools	93
Miscellaneous	94
Comprehensive Schools	95
Technical Schools	95
Bilateral and Multilateral Schools	97
Other Secondary Schools	97
Special Educational Treatment	97
DIRECT GRANT SCHOOLS	101
INDEPENDENT SCHOOLS	103
Registration	103
Recognition as Efficient	104
Nursery Schools	105
Independent Primary Schools	105
Pre-preparatory Schools	106

CONTENTS

Preparatory Schools	106
Independent Secondary Schools	108
Public Schools	108
Other Independent Schools	111
The Public Schools Commission	111
(iii) SUMMARY	113

5 EXAMINATIONS 116

11 +	116
The Tests	116
Who Uses What	120
COMMON ENTRANCE	121
The Questions	124
GENERAL CERTIFICATE OF EDUCATION	128
The Papers	130
University Entrance	134
THE CERTIFICATE OF SECONDARY EDUCATION	135
The Papers	137

6 CHOICE – AND FEE-PAYING 140

PARENTAL CHOICE IN THE STATE SYSTEM	140
Keeping the Child at Home	147
CHOICE AMONG INDEPENDENT SCHOOLS	148
HOW TO JUDGE A SCHOOL	148
PAYING FOR EDUCATION	153

7 MEDICAL AND OTHER SPECIAL SERVICES 157

MEALS AND MILK	157
CLOTHING AND CLEANSING	158
MEDICAL AND DENTAL INSPECTIONS	158

8 EDUCATIONAL CONTROVERSIES 160

CO-EDUCATION	160
BOARDING SCHOOLS	163
NURSERY SCHOOLS	169
STAYING ON AT SCHOOL	170

CONTENTS

STREAMING	171
FAMILY GROUPING	172

9 FURTHER AND HIGHER EDUCATION — 173

(i) THE PUBLIC SECTOR	174
Technical Colleges	174
Regional Colleges	175
National Colleges	175
Other Establishments	176
C.A.T.s and Polytechnics	176
Qualifications in Technical Colleges	177
Operatives, Apprentices, and Technicians	177
National Certificates and Diplomas	178
C.N.A.A. and other Degrees	179
The Industrial Training Act, 1964	180
County Colleges	183
Adult Education	183
The Youth Service	184
Colleges of Education	184
The Open University	185
(ii) THE UNIVERSITIES	186
Oxford and Cambridge	186
Scottish Universities	187
London and Wales	187
Civic Universities	188
New Universities	189
Former C.A.T.s	189
Independence and Money	190
University Degrees	191
(iii) THE ROBBINS REPORT	193
(iv) THE JAMES REPORT	194
Appendix 1 Books and Publications	195
Appendix 2 Educational Organizations	196
Appendix 3 Officials of an Education Authority	198
Appendix 4 What a Local Authority Spends	199
Glossary of Educational Terms	205
Index	221

Preface

EDUCATION is a very big industry. Every year 900,000 or so children are born in Great Britain, and helping them to grow and mature is the task of education. Its annual turnover is nearly £3,000m., or over 6 per cent of the gross national product. This is nearly as much as the nation spends on consumer durables, more than is spent on defence, alcohol, or the national health service and nearly twice as much as on public housing. There are some 33,000 schools, nearly four dozen universities, about 750 major establishments of further education and nearly 7,000 evening institutes. Well over 400,000 people are employed as school teachers alone: Britain has more teachers than soldiers, and there are more teachers here than there are Whites in Rhodesia.

What is more, the 'system' is the result of several centuries' haphazard growth and bristles with exceptions and anomalies. A sizeable number of schools (nearly 3,000) are independent and only very loosely affected by Acts and regulations. The statutory system itself has been described as 'a national service, locally administered' – and this means in practice that what happens on one side of a county boundary may be vastly different from what happens on the other. The universities are not directly controlled by the Department of Education – they get their government grants through the University Grants Committee. Scotland and Northern Ireland are laws unto themselves.

To keep this book within reasonable bounds, therefore, it has been decided to limit it to England and Wales, and to concentrate largely on schools and the administrative structure behind them. There is an outline of further and higher education, but a detailed treatment of these topics deserves a book to itself.

The hope is that the book will be a handy guide through the confusion. Increasing numbers of people are coming to need one. Their aspirations for education often outstrip the country's provision of it. Parents who themselves knew only state schools

PREFACE

are becoming interested in independent schools – and vice versa. There are many groups, parental and otherwise, who seek to improve what there is. It is for this reason that the section on administration (Chapter 3) is included and at such length. If a parent is trying to make the most of what there is in education, he will need to be aware of how the whole thing is run and who is responsible for what. For example, it is at best wasteful to be angry with a headmaster for something which really requires you to harry the Secretary of State for Education and Science.

Another consequence of the variety of institutions and the autonomy of local authorities is that it is almost impossible to describe anything acceptably in general terms. Claims for diversity can be overdone. Teachers and education officers often tend to overestimate the extent to which they are unique. Education in England and Wales is diverse, in the sense that the experience of individual parents can be markedly different from one area to another and in different parts of the same area. It is homogeneous in that the pattern of provision (or lack of it), the various stages of education, the kind of things taught, the examinations taken, are all broadly similar. But the only generalization that one educationist will allow another is that you cannot make generalizations about English education. I believe the picture given in this book is substantially accurate. But there are bound to be people who can justly claim that what is said about a group of schools does not apply to *their* school, which is in the group, and there are bound to be authorities who can also claim that, whatever might be true of most bodies, it isn't true of them.

There is one further difficulty, which can be overcome only by an arbitrary decision on the part of the author. What should one call those schools which are part of the statutory system of education? 'Local authority schools' is too cumbersome and does not allow for the influence of national policy. 'County and voluntary schools' is what they are called in the Education Act, 1944, but that is too much of a mouthful too. 'Maintained schools' is official but confusing. The obvious name should be 'public schools' – because that is what they are, and the term neatly begs the question of who has the most control over them. But it has already been pre-empted by schools which are not

PREFACE

in the least public, whatever else they are. We are left with the term 'state schools'. People in education often object violently to this on the ground that it implies a more uniform system than we actually have. It also has totalitarian overtones. I have decided to use it none the less for three reasons: it is brief; most people understand it and use it; 'state' implies to me the whole national and local apparatus of democratically controlled public authorities.

Finally, it is impossible to write a handbook without being enormously indebted to others. In the first place there are the reference books, official and unofficial, which appear in Appendix One. One of these must be especially mentioned: *The New Law of Education* by Taylor and Saunders. It is a marvellous guide to the jungle of educational law and is very readable too. A great deal of what one knows comes from people rather than books, and people in education are normally extraordinarily ready to share their knowledge and experience. I am particularly grateful to Dr L. F. W. White, Mr Noel Hughes, Miss Barbara Rees, Mr Eric E. Robinson and officials in the Department of Education. I am also grateful for the help of the county treasurer of Hampshire, Mr J. R. Sampson, in providing the revised form 501 F which appears as Appendix Four. Thanks are due too to the Advisory Centre for Education for permission to draw on material from the journal *Where?* – particularly the glossary and chapters on Choice and Controversies. As every journalist knows the Information Division of the Department of Education is extremely helpful: its help on this book has been incalculable. I hope there are no mistakes – but if there are, they are my fault.

The enormous amount of typing for this book was shared by Miss Sheila Bland, Mrs Noel Parsons and Mrs Shirley Fisher. Mrs Eve Sears revised the statistics for this edition and helped with the page proofs. To all of them I am very grateful. My parents' help in correcting typescripts is the very least of their relentless efforts on my behalf. This book is for them because they would probably have bought it even if it had been written by someone else.

CHAPTER ONE

People and Education

For most of us the only continuous connection we have with schools and colleges is when we ourselves are pupils and students. Naturally children, and even most students, are aware only of the institutions which they themselves attend. The class or form teacher or house master probably occupies the foreground of their view of school and the head teacher can easily remain a rather vague figure, even when he claims to know every child by name. For children 'school' is what happens to them. They are rarely, if ever, conscious that their particular school is just one of many, or that other schools may be quite different from their own. Still less do they realize the complicated administrative structure behind it. Why should they? Most of us retain this limited and innocent view of schools and education for the rest of our lives. The next time we see schools is when we ourselves are parents, and our knowledge is usually second-hand – through our children. A very few of us might actually visit the school for open days and concerts or, even more rarely, to consult the head teacher about our children. The more belligerent of us might storm into school in order to threaten a teacher with violence. The most that can be assumed is that however tenuous our connection with schools, we are probably uneasily aware that they have changed a lot since we were there.

Some really adventurous – normally comparatively rich – spirits actually assume that they ought to choose schools and try to inform themselves about alternatives. Equally adventurous but rather less rich people try to choose among state schools. In both cases the parent is likely to bump up against the administrative structure, the regulations and controls, of which he was previously only vaguely aware. If a parent has a dispute with the school or local authority he finds himself going very thoroughly into the whole administrative organization. Who, he wants to know, has the power to do what? One of the most interesting developments of the last few years has been the spontaneous formation of local groups for the 'advancement of state education'. These groups, like some parents' associations, find themselves of necessity making a detailed study of schools and of the education 'system', from the Department of Education and Science downwards.

Considering the indifference with which most of us regard schools and the education service, it is worth saying immediately that parents have duties towards their children specially placed on them by Act of Parliament. Under the Education Act, 1944 (the foundation of the modern education service), the duty of seeing that a child gets full-time education is placed squarely on the parents. To be precise, Section 36 of the Act says, 'It shall be the duty of the parent of every child of compulsory school age to cause him to receive efficient full-time education suitable to his age, ability and aptitude, either by regular attendance at school or otherwise.' In practice this means that parents must not only see that their children get efficient education: they must also, if the child is at a school, see that he attends regularly. The education service exists first to make it possible for the parent to discharge his duty by supplying suitable schools, and secondly, to ensure that he does so. Recalcitrant or incompetent parents are likely, therefore, to come up against the local education authority when they find themselves prosecuted for not sending their children to school. Anxious, ambitious, or simply interested parents are likely to come across the authorities when they want to choose or to change schools. All of us need to know not only about schools but also precisely what arrangment we have collectively made through Parliament to enable us to carry out the duties we have (also through Parliament) imposed upon ourselves.

CHAPTER TWO

The Law: The Education Act, 1944

EDUCATION in England and Wales is regulated by the Education Act, 1944, which received the Royal Assent on 3 August of that year. The Act was the culmination of an extraordinarily widespread and insistent demand for educational reform which accompanied the fighting of the second world war. Part of this demand arose when the children who were brought to light by evacuation were seen to have been reared in ignorance and squalor. Another influence came from the armed forces, where a lot of able men who had had only an elementary education were discovered. And the social idealism which accompanied the last years of the war demanded an end to the injustices of the thirties, and in particular insisted that children should not miss an education through parental circumstances.

Even so, nobody knows quite how the demand arose or why it should have been met so effectively. A similar agitation in the previous world war was nowhere near so widespread, and the 1918 Education Act was far less sweeping. In the early 1940s the Board of Education was lucky in having as President Mr R. A. Butler and as Parliamentary Secretary Mr J. Chuter Ede. In response to the demand for reform the Board, in 1941, sent out some draft proposals in a document called the 'green book' after the colour of its cover. The Board was flooded with replies from all kinds of organizations concerned with education, and agitation began in earnest. There sprang up a Council for Educational Advance – supported chiefly by the National Union of Teachers, the Workers' Educational Association, and the Trades Union Congress – to campaign for reform. Mr Butler and Mr Ede consulted and negotiated for months. Eventually, in 1943, they presented to Parliament a White Paper, called *Educational Reconstruction*, which became the basis for the new Act.

On the purely educational proposals there was little disagreement. 'Secondary education for all', for example, had graduated from being a revolutionary slogan of the infant Labour Party to

THE LAW: THE EDUCATION ACT, 1944

being a reasonable national aim. What argument there was, was about the position of denominational schools. It says an enormous amount for the patience and skill of Mr Butler and Mr Ede (as well as for the pacifying effects of war) that denominational and doctrinal wrangles did not bedevil this Education Bill as they had its predecessors. Some indication of the dangers can be gained from the fact that criticisms of the 'religious' clauses – during the passage of the Bill through Parliament – were usually met by the plea that to alter any particular proposal would upset the delicately poised negotiated settlement.

WHAT THERE WAS BEFORE

Before 1944 English education was the result of a haphazard accumulation of inadequacies over the centuries.

Secondary Education

The most historic institutions were the independent grammar schools. These had been founded, often in the Middle Ages (one of them claimed descent from Alfred the Great) through monasteries or cathedrals, or by city companies, monarchs, and other wealthy patrons. Under the influence of Dr Arnold in the last century some of them became 'public' boarding schools with national reputations. These remained independent because their endowments were large and their pupils' parents wealthy. Others were assisted or taken over entirely by the county and county borough councils. After 1902 the councils could establish their own secondary schools, so that by 1939 there were few towns of any size without one. Vocational education was given in technical schools and colleges established since the Technical Instruction Act of 1889. In some areas junior technical schools, taking children between 13 and 16, prepared pupils for a particular industry or industries, but vocational education was chiefly given in colleges for pupils over 16 years of age. In any case, even government committees disagreed between the wars on whether technical schools were really 'secondary' or not.

WHAT THERE WAS BEFORE

Elementary education

Elementary education was started by denominational and philanthropic bodies in the nineteenth century. They soon found it impossible to raise enough money by voluntary subscriptions and school fees, and from 1833 the State made annual grants and took powers to inspect the assisted schools. Locally elected school boards with the duty to establish schools where they were needed and the power to raise money by a rate were set up in 1870, and in 1880 attendance at school was made compulsory for every child. The provision of schools both by the denominations and by the boards was the foundation of the 'dual system' of control – vestiges of which are still with us. School fees were finally abolished in elementary schools in 1918. The Board of Education was created in 1899, and in 1902 the duties of the school boards were taken over by the councils of counties and county boroughs and of certain boroughs and urban districts. The 'board schools' became 'council schools'. The 1918 Education Act, which raised the age of compulsory school attendance to 14, required some provision to be made for practical and advanced instruction in elementary schools.

As early as 1926 the Consultative Committee of the Board of Education recommended the reorganizing of elementary schools into primary schools for children under 11 and senior or 'modern' schools for children over that age. The idea was that the school-leaving age should go up to 15 and that the senior schools should offer an alternative form of secondary education to that given in the grammar schools. This reform was held up by the fact that the denominations could not afford to build senior schools and the Board could neither compel them nor help them from rates or taxes to do so. (The denominations could not afford to keep their elementary schools up to modern standards either.) Even if the councils built new secondary schools there was no way of compelling the denominational elementary schools to send on their pupils at 11. Even the 1936 Act, by which the councils could give up to three-quarters of the cost of new denominational senior schools in return for more control over appointing teachers, was not as successful as had been hoped. In 1939 over half of the

THE LAW: THE EDUCATION ACT, 1944

elementary schools were denominational. Clearly the legislators of 1943 and 1944 had to remove denominational objections in order to make educational advance possible.

WHAT THE ACT DID

To the children of the country the main promise of the Act was free secondary education for all. This promise and the effort to bring together existing educational services meant changes in administration, in school organization and in the state's relations with religious bodies. The title of the Act was 'to reform the law relating to education in England and Wales' and it introduced the most sweeping changes in that law since the Act of 1870. It replaced and reformed almost all previous law relating to education.

Hitherto educational law had had social, as much as educational, objectives, emphasizing the protection of children rather than the promotion of education beyond the elementary stage. Fixing a compulsory school age, for example, was traditionally designed to keep children out of the hands of unscrupulous employers. The 1944 Act was by comparison educational, indeed almost child-centred, in outlook, enacting that children should be educated suitably for their ages, abilities, and aptitudes.

The main changes it made can be briefly summarized:

1) It created a Minister of Education and charged him with the duty positively to 'promote the education of the people of England and Wales' (see pages 25–44 and 53–62).

2) It made the county and the county borough councils the local authorities for education and gave them their powers and duties for education (see pages 51–8 and 62–3).

3) It reorganized education in three 'progressive' stages, known as primary (for pupils up to 12), secondary (for pupils over 12 and under 19), and further (for pupils of any age after leaving school). The compulsory school age was raised to 15 – and it may be raised to 16 without further legislation. Fees were abolished in maintained schools (see pages 65–97).

WHAT THE ACT DID

4) Denominational schools were brought into the state system as 'aided' or 'controlled' schools. A daily act of worship and regular religious instruction were made compulsory in state primary and secondary schools (see pages 74–6).

5) It made registration and inspection of independent schools compulsory from a date to be specified (see pages 103–111).

6) It gave the local authorities certain welfare functions – medical inspection, free medical and dental treatment, 'milk, meals, and other refreshments', clothing (if need be), board and lodging for necessitous children, and clothing for physical training for any children (see pages 157–9).

7) It made the local education authorities responsible for the special education of handicapped children (see pages 97–101).

8) It enabled local authorities to pay fees for pupils at fee-paying schools, to grant scholarships and awards for further and higher education, and to pay maintenance grants for children in state schools (see pages 153–6).

9) It gave the local authorities the duty to make arrangements for 'leisure-time occupation in organized cultural training and recreative activities' and to provide, after a date to be specified, compulsory part-time education equivalent to one day a week in 'county colleges' for those under 18 not getting other education (see page 183).

10) It required the local authorities to pay their teachers according to scales agreed by the Burnham Committee and approved by the Minister (see pages 70–72). It enacted equal pay for women (against the wish of the Government).

Legally, the provisions of the Act are now in operation, with two very important exceptions. The compulsory attendance of young people at county colleges will be delayed until the Minister decides to enforce it: that is, probably, for ever. The compulsory school age will be raised to 16 only in 1972–3.

It is worth noticing, too, what the Act did not cover. Its emphasis was on schools and statutory education. The universities were not considered part of the national education system

THE LAW: THE EDUCATION ACT, 1944

and they are still regarded as 'autonomous' institutions. Further education was thought to imply either evening classes or county colleges: the great development of the technical colleges was not foreshadowed in the Act.

There have been a number of little Acts since 1944 but they are mostly amending Acts only. They are the Education Act, 1946; the Education (Miscellaneous Provisions) Act, 1948; the Education (Miscellaneous Provisions) Act, 1953; the Education Act, 1959, which allowed the Minister to give more money to certain categories of voluntary schools; and the Education Act, 1962, which made new arrangements for grants to students and fixes two school-leaving dates a year instead of three. Children born between September and February, inclusive, leave at Easter; the rest at the end of the summer term. The Remuneration of Teachers Act, 1963, empowered the Minister to make one salary award in place of a Burnham award he had rejected. This Act was repealed by the Remuneration of Teachers Act, 1965, which set up new committees, on which the Secretary of State was represented, to consider teachers' salaries (see page 71). The Education Act, 1964, allowed local authorities to vary the age of transfer from primary to secondary schools and to pay maintenance grants to 15-year-olds in special schools. The Education Act, 1967, enabled the Secretary of State to make larger contributions (again) to voluntary schools. The Teachers' Superannuation Act, 1967, consolidated previous legislation. The Education Act, 1968, clarified the law on the effect of and procedure for changing the character of schools, and the Education (No. 2) Act, 1968, provided for more independent governing bodies of maintained colleges, particularly of colleges of education. The Education (Handicapped Children) Act, 1970, gave the Secretary of State responsibility for the education of the severely subnormal who had previously been excluded from school; and the Education (School Milk) Act, 1970, enabled local authorities to give milk to pupils of primary school age in middle schools. As this revision went to press the Education (Milk) Bill 1971 was going through Parliament: its object was to withdraw free milk for children over 7 and to enable local authorities to sell milk in primary and secondary schools.

WHAT THE ACT DID

By an order in Council of March 1964, the Minister of Education became the Secretary of State for Education and Science, and the Ministry became the Department of Education and Science. The Secretary of State and his Department have all the reponsibilities of the former Minister and Ministry, together with responsibility for the universities and civil science (see pages 24–6 and 190–91).

Most people in education would claim that the 1944 Act has been a great success. In support of this it must be said that the Act has been remarkably little amended. Most discussions about education take place in the context of its provisions. In 1971 the Secretary of State (Mrs Margaret Thatcher) said firmly, 'To enable us to advance as we would wish, major changes in the law are not necessary.' On the other hand, as Taylor and Saunders say, 'the ideals of 1944 remain unfulfilled ...', and they blame shortages of men and materials in the building industry; balance of payments crises restricting public expenditure; the post-war 'bulge' and more recent increases in the birth-rate; the unexpected shortage of teachers and local movements of population. At the same time, the Act is getting out of date. Its division of education into three stages has already been modified. Some of its detailed administrative provisions are proving inadequate, and there is a growing sense that the place of parents and teachers should be better recognized in educational legislation. In December 1968 it was announced that 'work is now in hand on the preparation of a new Education Bill. The aim is both to consolidate current legislation, with minor amendments which experience has shown to be necessary, and to make some desirable changes in the law.' Local authorities, teachers' organizations and others were invited to make their views known, and there was growing pressure for a new Act to replace the great measure of 1944. With the change of government in 1970 it became clear that there would be a consolidating Act rather than major legislation, so we can now turn to look in more detail at what education is like in England and Wales in 1971.

CHAPTER THREE

Administering Education

THE DEPARTMENT OF EDUCATION AND SCIENCE

Parliament

WHAT happens in education is ultimately the responsibility of Parliament. Parliament enacts legislation laying down the national policy for education and determining how it should be controlled and administered, votes most of the money spent on education and keeps a general watch through debates and Members' questions. The Secretary of State has a duty under the 1944 Act to make an annual report to Parliament giving an account of the way he has used the powers and duties conferred on him, and of the work of his Central Advisory Councils. This report, which is published by the Stationery Office (the one for 1970 cost 60p), always makes interesting reading, and is supplemented by separate volumes of statistics. Its publication is often the occasion for the annual full day's debate on education in the House of Commons. This is of course not the only time when the Minister may be called to account in Parliament. Both Government and Opposition may initiate debates on education. It is open to any M.P. to ask Parliamentary questions. The day set aside for oral answers from the Department of Education is Thursday, but written replies are published in the back of *Hansard* on any day. M.P.s may also initiate debates on the adjournment of the House when they feel a reply is unsatisfactory – or for some other reason. New Bills going through Parliament are of course fully debated. Like other Ministers, the Secretary of State for Education normally finds himself faced by a 'shadow' Minister, on the Opposition front bench, though naturally the Opposition's duties are much less formally defined. Both sides of the House have Parliamentary Education Groups. In each of the two big parties, about two dozen M.P.s specially interested in education meet regularly in the House to discuss education, to hear experts on particular topics, to question the Secretary of State on occasions privately, and generally to keep themselves informed. (One might add here too that the National Union of Teachers sponsors M.P.s on both sides of the House to keep their interests before Parliament.) The Secretary of State is a member of the Government (usually in the Cabinet) and a Member of Parliament – though he need not be in the House of Commons. Lord Hailsham, when Minister from January to September 1957, was a peer.

The Secretary of State

It was by the 1944 Act that Parliament created both a Minister and a Ministry of Education. The precise words (of Section 1, Sub-Section 1 of the Act) are worth quoting:

> It shall be lawful for His Majesty to appoint a Minister (hereinafter referred to as 'the Minister') whose duty it shall be to promote the education of the people of England and Wales and the progressive development of institutions devoted to that purpose, and to secure the effective execution by local authorities, under his control and direction, of the national policy for providing a varied and comprehensive educational service in every area.

Though they may not sound it, these are strong words, and the general power of controlling and directing local authorities in carrying out national policy is very much more definite than the mere power of 'superintendence' formerly given to the President of the Board of Education. The Minister is required actively to ensure, through his powers under the Act, that the local education authorities comply with government policy. Under Section 99 the Minister can force the local authority to discharge the duties placed on it by the Act. Section 68 even gives him the power to give such directions as he thinks fit if a local authority acts or proposes to act 'unreasonably'.

The Minister has now become a Secretary of State and has gained additional responsibilities. The universities have for several decades received their Government grants through an independently constituted University Grants Committee. Departmental responsibility for the U.G.C. was vested in the Treasury until 1963, and for a short time after that in the Lord President of the Council. In 1959 a Minister for Science had been appointed to coordinate Government responsibility for civil science. In 1964 the Department of Education and Science was created, in which were merged the functions of the former Minister of Education, of the Lord President and of the Minister for Science – except that a little later atomic energy and industrial research went to the Ministry of Technology.

The translation of Mr Butler, the last President of the Board of Education, into the first Minister of Education on 10 August 1944, was held at the time to be symbolic of a change of status for the political head of the department concerned with education. This was something of an illusion. The status of any Minister in the country depends upon the way he and his office are treated by the Government. One Minister of Education since the war, Miss Florence Horsbrugh (later Lady Horsbrugh), was not even in the Cabinet. In 1957 there were three different Ministers of Education and the office was commonly spoken of as a stepping stone to better things. When Sir David Eccles (now Lord Eccles) left the Ministry of Education in January 1957 to become a President (of the Board of Trade) this was widely thought to be promotion. But somewhere about that time people began to realize that the Ministry of Education was a department with huge responsibilities, spending a thousand million pounds a year, more than any other department except defence. So when Sir David Eccles returned to education in 1959 some people claimed he had been promoted again. Certainly when Mr Anthony Crosland moved in 1967, from the Department of Education and Science to the Board of Trade, nobody said this was promotion.

Whatever the Minister's status in the country and the Cabinet, his position in Education was certainly altered in 1944. He no longer, like the President of the Board, passively 'superintends': it is his duty to 'promote' the education of the people. Before 1944 it was the local authorities who had the chief power of initiative in education. The President could do little more than state minimum standards, enforce them through the grant regulations and, in circulars and through the inspectors, exhort the authorities to greater efforts. Now the Secretary of State can direct authorities to make improvements, and no authority can do much without his approval. What is more he is the arbiter in a dispute between an authority and parents or managers and governors. He may even direct an authority to establish, maintain, or assist a college of education. His responsibilities are wide and his powers great.

They are not, however, unlimited. In the first place, Ministers have not rushed to be energetic despots. Early on, in 1947, the school leaving age was raised to 15 (as laid down in the Act) against the wishes of most people in education, but this was rather an exotic show of force. Normally progress is expected to be made by consultation and agreement. This is partly because too much direction from the centre smacks of totalitarianism, partly because it is thought that local government is a good thing. Most of the money that is spent locally is spent on education, and the idea of local responsibility and control in education is carefully fostered. Educationists normally explain at some length the checks and balances which exist to preserve the freedom of individual teachers, schools, and local authorities. Formally, these may look rather flimsy, but the idea of a 'partnership' between central and local authorities helps to preserve a convention of decentralization.

In the second place the powers which the Act gives a Secretary of State are in a sense too great to be used. A local authority would have almost to go off its head before the Secretary of State was justified in using his powers against it. In the third place, some of his powers are more apparent than real. Many people, including at least one judge, have assumed that Section 1, Sub-Section 1 of the 1944 Act gives the Secretary of State extensive power. But general introductory sections of Acts have in themselves no legal consequences. He can act under Section one only in so far as he is given specific powers under later Sections. For example, when the Government decided, in 1964, that secondary education should be reorganized on comprehensive lines (see page 86) the then Secretary of State took pains to point out that he could not compel local authorities to reorganize. Most local authorities did submit schemes of reorganization, but this is evidence as much for a growing belief in the folly of selection at 11 plus as for the influence of the Secretary of State. In policy, he is not a despot: in administration – in school building, teachers' salaries and so on – his influence and that of his Department are increasingly pervasive.

The Secretary of State for Education, like other Ministers, is a 'corporation sole'. He is a corporate body in himself and is responsible for everything done in his name or by his agents. He is held in law, in other words, to do very much more than one man could possibly do, but he is personally accountable for what goes on in education, and if things go badly wrong he should in theory resign. (In these and later references to the Secretary of State, 'he' implies 'she' when, as in 1971, the Minister is a woman.)

The Secretary of State's Functions

Personally, the Secretary of State has three main functions. First he must decide policy and action. In formulating his policy he will obviously be influenced by the political philosophy he holds and the party to which he belongs. He may be committed by his party's election manifesto to a specific course of action, as Labour Secretaries of State were in 1964 to secondary reorganization. A particular Secretary of State may or may not have had some hand in formulating his party's policy (two Labour Secretaries of State since 1964 could be said to have done so). The British tradition of amateur government backed by professional civil servants means that the Secretary of State can be quite ignorant about his Department and its work until the day he is appointed, though it would be silly to underestimate how generally well informed leading politicians are. At all events, what he actually does will be much affected by his consultations with his colleagues in the Cabinet. In particular, he must compete, as a 'spending' Minister, with all the other 'spending' Ministers for the favour of the Chancellor of the Exchequer. There is a vicious circle which a resourceful Secretary of State must break. If education is held cheaply in the country it will not be well treated by the Government. If it is seen to be badly treated by the Government it will be held cheaply in the country.

This underlines the second personal function of the Secretary of State: to be a spokesman for education in the country. He can do this by his speeches in Parliament and at his own party conferences and other functions. He has plenty of other opportunities too. Professional associations of educationists all have annual conferences and there are always schools and colleges to be opened. A Secretary of State finds that he has plenty of opportunity for speaking and proselytizing for education. The proportion of enthusiastic waffle to firm proposals for improvement is often disappointingly large, but three Ministers in the last decade have perceptibly raised the level of educational debate.

The third personal function of the Secretary of State is to look after his Department itself and all its complicated dealings with Parliament, the public, the professional associations and the local authorities.

The Secretary of State also functions as a member of the Government and of the Cabinet. This means he must read and think about subjects which are nothing to do with his own Department or only marginally relevant to it. The Secretary of State may be a member of a Cabinet Committee on, for example, Rhodesia, economic policy or regional development. He must work at these subjects, attend meetings and share decisions. When he does so he is not functioning as the spokesman of his Department, and he is unlikely to get any briefing from it. The better he is, the more likely he is to be a significant member of the Cabinet and thus to spend time on other things than education. All this became more evident when Sir Edward Boyle ceased to be Minister of Education in 1964. He became Minister of State (a junior Minister) in the enlarged Department, but remained in the Cabinet, in as it were a personal capacity.

Each Secretary of State has his own style, and this can affect the effectiveness and the morale of the Department, relations with local authorities and teachers, and the regard in which education is generally held. One or two have become intensely interested in the objectives and problems of education. Others have a primary interest elsewhere, in economic affairs for instance. One recent Minister gained a reputation for his skill in running the Ministry. Another was frankly lazy. Some are good at the competition in Cabinet with other spending Ministers: others are perhaps too aware of wider political and economic restraints. An occasional one has ideas of his own which he is determined to pursue: others seem simply to reflect the policies and attitudes of their civil servants. Even obvious incompetence is not unknown.

The Secretary of State's Day

Every Secretary of State differs – and so does every day – but he may typically get to his office about ten in the morning. From then until lunchtime he probably sees his private secretary about urgent correspondence or messages, and the permanent secretary and other high civil servants for discussions, to make decisions or to give them instructions on the preparation of a Cabinet paper. There may be meetings to be held, attended by a junior Minister and quite a number of civil servants, minutes and papers to be read, and deputations to be received. Most Cabinet meetings take place in the mornings. In the afternoons, the Secretary of State may attend the House of Commons: he will have to be there if it is his day for answering Parliamentary Questions. If the Government's majority is small, there will be many days when the Secretary of State is kept at the House of Commons all the time it is sitting, perhaps all night. He will probably be busiest when a Bill is being prepared for Parliament. Most Education Bills are quite small, but then they involve a great deal of preparation. Government amendments have to be settled and the Secretary of State's attitude to amendments by M.P.s and peers has to be decided. If the committee stage of the Bill is taken in standing committee these meetings will start at 10.30 in the morning, though much of this work may be done by a junior Minister. It is usually during the recess that the Secretary of State visits local authorities, colleges, and schools in various parts of the country or speaks at the conferences of educational associations.

Junior Ministers

Departmental Ministers normally have Parliamentary Under-Secretaries to assist them in their Departments and in the House of Commons. The Secretary of State for Education and Science has three junior Ministers, and one of them is a Minister of State.

CIVIL SERVANTS

A Minister of State has a status somewhere between that of a full Minister and a Parliamentary Under-Secretary. The office was a war-time invention and was used at first for *ad hoc* duties, like that of Mr Harold Macmillan in North Africa. Subsequently Ministers of State have been appointed in the Treasury and the Foreign Office, and the general idea is to create a Minister of a higher status than a Parliamentary Secretary to relieve heavily burdened departmental Ministers. In 1971 the Minister within the Department was the Paymaster General, with responsibility for the arts and libraries. The two Parliamentary Under-Secretaries of State were responsible for (i) schools, youth service and special education; (ii) higher and further education and teachers. The powers exercised by all junior Ministers are those of the Secretary of State, and the extent of their responsibilities is for him to decide.

The Secretary of State's Parliamentary Private Secretary is not a member of the Government. He is appointed by the Secretary of State (not by the Prime Minister) to be a two-way channel of information between the Secretary of State and back-bench M.Ps.

Civil Servants

The Department of Education and Science employs about 3,000 civil servants. At its head is the Permanent Under-Secretary of State, who in 1971 was Sir William Pile. He is responsible to the Secretary of State for the organization of the Department and for the advice it gives him. He is also personally responsible to the Secretary of State and the Treasury for the finance of the Department and has to answer for the Departmental accounts and estimates to the Public Accounts and Estimates Committees of the House of Commons. He has four Deputy Under-Secretaries (broadly for schools, higher and further education, arts and science), and below them are the Assistant Under-Secretaries or equivalent officers, each of whom is responsible for one or more of the branches into which the Department is divided.

The branches are not particularly static things. New ones are created and old ones reorganized. In 1971 the branches and their responsibilities were as follows.

Schools Branch deals with primary and secondary education. Territorial teams maintain contact with the local education authorities in a region. Much of their work is concerned with the school building programme (see page 38), but they also see that statutory requirements are met when schools are opened or closed and deal with cases of individual pupils referred to the Secretary of State. There are also functional teams dealing with the reorganization of secondary education, voluntary schools, religious education, direct grant and independent schools, curriculum, decimalization and metrication, race relations, education of immigrants, careers guidance, road safety, nursery education and welfare.

Special Education Branch is concerned with physically and mentally handicapped children. Medical Branch deals with the school health service and the nutritional aspects of school meals. The Principal Medical Officer and his staff are part of this branch which is organized in functional teams.

There are three branches dealing with teachers. Teachers Branch I deals with the long-term demand and supply of teachers (including recruiting publicity), administers the quota system, advises on the qualifications, probation and medical fitness of teachers, on conditions of service and salaries and on the application of Burnham reports. Teachers Branch II is responsible for teacher training, through the local authorities, universities and voluntary bodies which provide it. Functional teams deal with the curriculum, college government, recruitment and admissions to colleges, technical teacher training and courses for serving teachers, and training for the youth service. Teachers' Pensions Branch deals with the Administration of the Teachers' Superannuation Acts.

Further Education Branch has four main divisions. The first is responsible for higher education and is concerned with the development of colleges, the approval of advanced courses and public relations. The second deals with policy for the vocational education of craftsmen, operatives and technicians, with the consequences of the Industrial Training Act, with engineering and construction education and with examinations, particularly national certificates and diplomas. The third deals with vocational education in further education institutions in such areas as agriculture, management, librarianship, cartography, textiles and music and drama. It also deals with art education generally. The fourth deals with further education building programmes, national colleges and other direct grant establishments, visual aids in technical colleges and further education for overseas students.

Universities Branch is concerned with broad questions of university finance and policy and with policy on student grants. It administers postgraduate studentships in arts subjects, the mature state scholarship scheme and grants for students in colleges of education. It is also responsible for the Open University, for adult education and computers. As we shall see (page 190) capital and recurrent grants from the Government are distributed to individual universities by the University Grants Committee.

Science Branch provides the link between the Department and the Research Councils and the secretariat for the Council for Scientific Policy. It also deals with scientific representations abroad, scientific relations with foreign missions in London and participation in the scientific activities of international organizations like O.E.C.D., N.A.T.O., U.N.E.S.C.O. and the Council of Europe, and with technical information in science and technology in the United Kingdom.

A number of branches in the Department provide specialized services and information. Architects and Building Branch deals with building policy and procedures, the scrutiny and approval of building projects (other than university) and research in building design and techniques. Finance Branch deals with control and planning of education expenditure (other than university), prepares estimates of local authority expenditure in connection with the rate support grant and makes all payments for the Department. Planning and Programmes Branch investigates implications, for money, manpower and other resources, of educational plans, and runs the Department's statistical services and educational research programme. Legal Branch not only gives legal advice; it drafts minor legislation, does preparatory work for Bills and has jurisdiction over educational charities. Establishments and Organization Branch is responsible for the organization, staffing and accommodation of the Department.

The Arts and Libraries Branch deals with the export of works of art, works of art generally, national museums and galleries, the Arts Council, Covent Garden, the National Theatre and other institutions, the administration of the Public Libraries and Museums Act of 1964, and the national libraries policy and all general policy matters relating to libraries.

The External Relations and General Branch is responsible for the administration of school meals, cooperation internally and with other Government departments, representation of D.E.S. interests under multilateral and bilateral international agreements, implications for the education service in the U.K.'s joining the European Economic Community, international education visits and exchanges, and includes the Press Office, publications, films etc.

The Education Office for Wales in Cardiff is not, strictly, a branch. It has its own permanent under-secretary, though he ranks as an assistant under-secretary. It advises on the application to Wales of policies being considered by other branches. It gives Welsh education authorities and other organizations a special approach to the Department and it is responsible for the administration in Wales of nursery, primary and secondary education.

The divisions in each branch, or the territorial or specialist teams, are headed by assistant secretaries. Below them are principals and executive and clerical officers. The assistant secretaries are the most senior people normally engaged in day-to-day administration. Above them it is all policy. In fact one distinguished civil servant has said that above assistant secretary level you don't have a job. A territorial principal deals with one or more local authorities. It is to him that the authorities write, and he decides whether a project or a proposal conforms with the regulations or with policy. It is he who first sees complaints or appeals by parents against 'his' authorities. Any decision which he cannot take himself will be referred to his assistant secretary, and it might go right up through the hierarchy to the Secretary of State. If this happens, the decision comes right down the line to the territorial principal, who then writes to the authority.

There are nearly 150 people in the Department from permanent under-secretary to trainee principals, all of them in the administrative grade of the civil service. There are also over 370 professional officers – lawyers, doctors, accountants, architects – a few of whom are in charge of the appropriate branches. The other 2,400 civil servants are in the executive, clerical and other grades. The Secretary of State's own staff is called the Secretariat. (It used to be called the Private Office, and this is the name most people still use.) It consists of a principal, a higher executive officer, a personal assistant, and clerks. The Secretariat acts as the main channel of communication between the Secretary of State and his Department. It arranges for the Department to provide briefs for meetings and draft letters, papers, and notes for speeches; and for transmitting the Secretary of State's instructions, slants on policy, and relevant personal views. A strong private secretary is often a key person in the Department next to the permanent under-secretary. He is the Secretary of State's confidant and knows a lot of secrets. It is a plum job for a principal.

Senior appointments in the Department are theoretically made by the Secretary of State. In practice Ministers play little part, so as to avoid political bias and charges of favouritism. The Prime Minister's formal (and sometimes real) approval is required for some posts, and the head of the Treasury really decides appointments at permanent under-secretary level. The main offices of the Department of Education are in the heart of Mayfair, in Curzon Street, London W1. The office of the Paymaster-General is in Belgrave Square.

Policy and Practice

The Secretary of State does not, of course, formulate policy all on his own. Naturally he will make known early in his career the broad outlines he wishes the Department to follow. But he will expect his civil servants to comment on his ideas and contribute to them. Any ideas he has for policy or action will be the subject of a minute to the permanent under-secretary or a junior Minister. He may call for information or reports on particular questions, or give directions. A great many points of policy will be initiated by the civil servants themselves and in this case the Secretary of State is the man who decides on what has been put before him. Although the civil servants are not themselves politicians they must know a great deal about politics. Any scheme they put up should at least avoid getting the Secretary of State into trouble in the House of Commons and the country.

What the Department does

Many people find it difficult to imagine what senior civil servants actually do. Perhaps the most readily understandable activity – because the result is obvious – is the preparation of a Bill or a White Paper. The civil servants in the Department will have consultation after consultation with interested parties. With Bills they will work out how the Department wants the law changed and draft papers for the Cabinet. They will brief the Minister taking the Bill through the House. But the Bill itself and all Government amendments are drafted by Parliamentary Counsel, who come under the Lord Chancellor. On the White Paper on polytechnics published in 1966 civil servants consulted over 1,000 organizations and individuals. A similar process of consultations goes on before the Secretary of State issues regulations.

Even so, the Secretary of State and his civil servants do not spend most of their time on legislation or even on settling big issues of policy. Most of the Department's work is day-to-day administration. It will involve discussing and settling small difficulties. Answering a Parliamentary question may take a principal a whole day or more. When the Secretary of State has to act as arbiter between a parent or a group of parents and a local authority, he and his civil servants will spend a great deal of time on details which may have important repercussions.

When one gets a letter from the Department of Education it may very well begin, 'I am directed by the Secretary of State for Education and Science to . . .' This is an example of his complete responsibility for everything that is done in his name. The chance that he has actually seen the letter, or directed the writer, is remote.

The work of the Department is conducted normally by

conference and minutes. Minutes are observations or reports, with perhaps recommendations for action or inaction. Very often a whole file may be built up as a minute emerges from the comparative obscurity of a principal through the hierarchy to the Secretary of State. This business of civil servants sending notes to each other is often derided – but it is part of the price we pay for parliamentary democracy and Ministerial accountability.

Some idea of the work of the Department of Education can be gained from the activities already described. Its breadth and variety make it impossible to sum up briefly, but a few examples may help.

Money One way the Department influences what is spent on education, and how, is through the grants of money made by the Government to the local authorities. In this the position of the Department is at least as anomalous as the whole set-up.

The money spent on education comes from three main sources: taxes; rates; endowments, fees, contributions, and so on. The first two of these are by far the most important. The actual spending is done mostly by the local authorities, the Government's contribution (some 55 per cent) being made in the form of a general grant of money. The Government's contribution, however, is not made through the Department of Education, but through the Department of the Environment. This is because the Government gives a total sum (called a 'rate support grant') to each local authority to spend on all its local government services, of which education is only one, though the biggest. It is up to the local authority to decide how much of the block grant shall be spent on education. It is in the negotiations between the two Departments (Education and the Environment) on the one hand, and the Association of Municipal Corporations, the County Councils Association, and the Greater London Council on the other, that the Department of Education influences in so far as it can, the total amount spent on education.

The total sums agreed in the negotiations of 1970 were £3,795m. for 1971–2 and £3,970m. for 1972–3. These sums formed the basis on which the rate support grant for the two years was fixed by the Secretary of State for the Environment. The method of determining the total of rate support grant is to calculate the aggregate Exchequer grant by applying a percentage to the negotiated amounts and deducting therefrom the amount of grants earmarked to specific services. The aggregate amount of Exchequer grants were £2,182m. for 1971–2 and £2,303m. for 1972–3 representing 57½ per cent and 58 per cent of the total respectively. The amount of grants earmarked to specific services were £178m. and £187m. for 1971–2 and 1972–3 respectively. Thus the totals of rate support grant were fixed at £2,004m. for the first year and £2,116m. for the second. If an authority spent the agreed amount it got the agreed contribution from the Government. If it spent more, the extra money had to come from the rates. The amount of the totals devoted to education was agreed as £2,055m. in 1971–2 and £2,148m. for 1972–3, so education takes over half of the local authorities' total expenditure. The negotiations are not wholly painless. Local authorities have complained that the Departments' estimates allow too little for existing commitments, let alone for expansion.

The Department's own expenditure for the year 1969–70 was £67m., of which £15m. was on capital grants to voluntary schools, colleges of education and technological institutions and so on. The current expenditure was mainly on grants to institutions. The Department's staff and Her Majesty's Inspectors cost £6.4m.

Building The Secretary of State's control over building is much more direct than it is over finance. As even Government committees have found this control and its relationship to the grant-making arrangements confusing, it is as well to try and make it all clear from the start. The amount of rate support grant is estimated by negotiation two years in advance, and estimates of the amount of likely building are of course taken into account. But the actual proposals for building still have to be submitted by the local authorities to the Department; its power to approve or reject them derives from the Government's control over capital investment in the public sector. When a local authority's proposals have been approved, the authority finds the money for them from loans financed from the agreed rate support grant and the rates.

The local education authorities submit their building plans for primary and secondary schools and for further education to the Secretary of State, who approves or rejects them according to government policy and the comparative needs of various authorities. Recently the authorities have been encouraged to compile annual building programmes farther ahead and the procedure for approval of projects has been streamlined. There are two chief classes of project: major works or minor works. The names are fairly self-explanatory. Minor works are projects costing up to about £40,000 (you could build three permanent classrooms or a school hall for this) and major works are anything bigger.

The argument for having two classes of project is that if a complete new school (a major work) is built it is marvellous for the people affected but not at all helpful to anybody else. The purpose of the minor works programme is to make it possible to relieve some of the more appalling hardships in schools which are not due to be rebuilt. It is possible, for example, to civilize the lavatories, lay an extra playground, or convert rooms into laboratories as part of a minor works programme.

Even after they have been agreed, these building programmes are vulnerable to shifts in Government policy, and especially to economic crisis measures. In 1968, after a decision to postpone the raising of the school leaving age, the major building programme for 1968–9 was docked by £29m. and thrown into little short of chaos. Normally, however, it is the minor works programme which suffers – or gains the odd windfall from an attempt to relieve unemployment.

The study and approval of building programmes is a major activity of the Department, but it is not the only method of control. The Department lays down minimum standards for school building and maximum limits to the costs per place. This has encouraged local authorities to design schools efficiently, though some of the laggards who were still committed to the pre-war neo-Georgian style have sometimes found themselves squeezed by the minimum standards and maximum costs to the point where they almost could not build. Overall, however, the costs of school building have been drastically reduced since the war.

In 1950, for example, the primary school cost limit was £170 a place. This would have been over £250 at 1963 prices, but the limit in that year was actually £175. In 1971 it was £257. And we have been getting better schools at the same time. Effective teaching space, for example, has gone up from, say, 21 to 26 sq. ft a cost place in 1951 to 23 to 30 sq. ft today.

The Department has done more, however, than simply lay down standards and limits. The development group of the architects and building branch, begun in 1949, has already done a great deal of research into building methods and into the uses to which schools are actually put. The results of their studies have been published in building bulletins, issued regularly, which the local authorities and their architects can study. The Department's architects have been almost unique in studying over a long period the needs of the actual users of the buildings they were concerned with. Many forward-looking authorities, like Nottinghamshire, Buckinghamshire, and Hertfordshire, have profited from this approach and have cooperated with the Department's architects.

When a school needs new buildings, large or small, what normally happens is that the existing inconvenience and squalor moves the head, staff, and perhaps parents and managers or governors, to complain to the local education authority. The local authority considers the matter and puts its own proposals to the governors and head; if there is agreement, the authority puts the project in one of its building programmes, usually a programme for two or three years ahead. The whole programme goes to the Minister, who will almost certainly cut it, probably by half. The individual project may or may not suffer in this. If it is cut out this time it will presumably go into the next programme, until it achieves priority. It is the local authority which is responsible for seeing that new schools are ready to meet rising populations or new housing estates.

Independent Schools Since 1957, Part III of the 1944 Act has been in force, and all independent schools have had to be registered with the Department of Education and Science. In addition, schools may apply to be recognized as efficient. This is discussed fully on pages 103–5. At the end of 1970 the register of independent schools contained 1,232 finally registered schools (besides

POLICY AND PRACTICE

the 1,409 recognized as efficient). There were also 54 provisionally registered schools of which 31 had come into existence during the year. Some 38 schools were added to the register and 165 removed on closure or change of status. The Secretary of State served 10 notices of complaint during the year, making 191 since 1957, for deficiencies in premises, accommodation, instruction, or individual teachers. Of these 2 cases went to the Independent Schools Tribunal. The Secretary of State also dealt with 12 schools where the time limit for satisfying his requirements had expired. Seven of these schools eventually met the requirements: the rest were struck off the register or their premises disqualified from being used as a school, or both.

In 1967 the Secretary of State announced that he would apply the standards required for recognition as efficient to all registered boarding schools. In 1971 this policy was modified: the Secretary of State is seeking to ensure a rise in standards as a condition of registration, but without making recognition standards obligatory.

What the Department does not do

It might be as well to note here what the Department does not do. It does not directly control the universities. These are independent bodies, and such money as they get from the Government is given through the University Grants Committee. Education in approved schools and Borstal institutions comes under the Home Office, and education in the services is controlled by the service departments. The Department does not itself directly own, establish or control any school. It does not control the selection, appointment, or promotion of teachers, nor does it pay them directly. It does not prepare, publish nor distribute textbooks, neither does it decide if, how or when any particular subject should be taught in schools. (There is one weird exception to this: the 1944 Act lays down the amount and nature of religious instruction to be given in schools – see pages 75–6.) It does not directly control museums, art galleries or public libraries – except by an odd chance, the Science, Victoria and Albert, Bethnal Green and Wellington Museums, Ham House and Osterley Park House.

Consultation and Advice

Regulations, Circulars and Memoranda The Secretary of State for Education and Science makes known his policies and requirements in a number of ways. Under the 1944 Act he tells local authorities what he wants in the way of organization and administration and the conditions on which grants will be paid in what are called statutory rules, regulations and instruments. These give precision and detail to brief and general requirements of the Act. They have the force of law: if a local authority or other body fails to comply with them, the Secretary of State might refuse to authorize the Exchequer's share of the cost of the service involved; in an extreme situation he could take over control from the body concerned.

These regulations are second in importance only to the the Act. For example, the Schools Regulations, 1959 (which replaced earlier, similar regulations), govern the repair of school premises, the size of classes, admission to schools, the length of the school year, school terms and holidays and the school day, and the appointment and qualifications of teachers. It was in these regulations and not in the Act itself that the famous recommendation on the size of classes used to appear. Under this regulation the number of pupils in class should be below thirty in secondary schools and below forty in primary schools. In practice, class sizes had been diminishing steadily if slowly, and in 1969 this regulation was revoked. The formal safeguard of minimum staffing standards now rests in another regulation, 'that there shall be in every school a staff of assistant teachers suitable and sufficient in number to provide full-time education appropriate to the ages, abilities and aptitudes of the pupils.'

Another good example of the detailed importance of statutory rules and regulations is offered by the Standards for School Premises Regulations, 1959. These lay down, for instance, that the site of a primary school with between twenty-six and fifty pupils shall not be less than five-eighths of an acre, that the site of every primary school shall include 'a paved area, laid on suitable foundations, properly graded and drained and suitable for activities to be carried out thereon . . .' and that every primary school other than an infant school shall have playing-field accommodation appropriate to the number of pupils. The regulations also cover teaching accommodation, staff-rooms, lavatories, cloak-rooms, wash-basins, and so on, for both primary and secondary schools.

Another way in which the Minister can make known his policies and wishes is by circulars, memoranda, and the like. Many circulars simply explain statutory instruments or otherwise relate to duties imposed by the Education Acts. Circulars and memoranda are not legally binding in themselves, but normally what the circulars say goes. The difference is that the local authorities can argue with a circular: all they can do with a regulation is induce the Minister to bring out a new one. One of the most famous pseudo-circulars is the *Manual of Guidance Schools No. 1*. This deals with the principles governing the parent's right to choose a school (see pages 140–47).

The most famous recent circulars have been Circular 10/65 and Circular 10/70. These are discussed in full on pages 86–92. Briefly, Circular 10/65 asserted the then Government's policy for reorganizing secondary education on comprehensive lines. It added that the Secretary of State requested local authorities to prepare and submit plans for doing so and listed the kinds of schemes that would be acceptable. After the change of Government in 1970, Circular 10/70 announced that the earlier circular was withdrawn. The point to note here is that none of this had the force of law. Several local authorities refused to act on the first circular, and virtually none of the large majority who were reorganizing altered their plans as a result of the second.

The most numerous documents which the Minister publishes are administrative memoranda. These are normally about matters of routine, but some are much more than this. The 'Notes for Guidance' to local authorities on the establishment of polytechnics was an administrative memorandum – No. 8/67. Most regulations, circulars and memoranda may be bought from the Stationery Office or through any bookseller.

All these Ministerial documents are not composed solely by the people in Curzon Street and launched on an entirely unsuspecting educational world. Both content and wording are discussed by Department officials, local authorities, teachers' associations, and other professional bodies. Normally it is hoped that a regulation will be an agreed document by the time it is published – though of course the Minister always has the final say. Unanimity about circulars is not so important, though the same sort of consultation goes on.

The Inspectorate With whom is all this consultation done? Most day-to-day consultation takes place with Her Majesty's Inspectors (the H.M.I.s). The inspectorate is attached to the Department, but inspectors have something of a special status. Their independence is emphasized and valued. But they cannot pursue policies out of line with the Secretary of State's and their ability to comment on ministerial policy is much the same as that of other civil servants. Posts in the inspectorate are advertised and are normally filled by ex-teachers. The senior chief inspector is the head of the inspectorate and he is responsible to the permanent under-secretary. Below him are six chief inspectors who each supervise one particular aspect of education: primary education, educational developments and special educational treatment, secondary education, further education connected with industry and commerce, other further education, the training of teachers. Based at the Department, too, are the staff inspectors. Each of these specializes in some particular aspect of education: for example, the teaching of the various school subjects (like classics or geography), the various stages of education (primary, further education, and so on), liaison with other Ministries or with overseas countries and organizations, building, or the youth service. For inspection purposes, England is divided into ten divisions (Wales is a division in itself) and each division into districts. A divisional inspector is responsible for each division and an inspector is allotted to each district. Altogether there are roughly 550 H.M.I.s.

The most obvious thing the inspectors do is to inspect all schools – state and independent – in their areas, as well as technical, art, and commerce colleges, colleges of education, the youth service, and adult education. They review and report on the content and value of the education given in the schools, and

POLICY AND PRACTICE

they may do this either by individual visits or by a full inspection in which a team of specialist inspectors descend on a school or college for several days. Their reports may be highly complimentary or heavily critical – in both cases they are confidential. Here is one example of the former and two of the latter:

A spirit of earnest and sustained endeavour characterizes the work as a whole. The pupils are keen to take advantage of the opportunities offered to them, they are whole-hearted in their application to the tasks in hand, and they present their written work neatly and systematically. For their part, the teachers interpret the syllabuses in a liberal and enlightened way. Much skilful teaching enlists the active co-operation of the pupils and ensures that they make their full contributions to the lessons. In many subjects recording and note making are, in the main, the pupils' responsibility; discussion is encouraged and stimulated; the preparation and reading of papers is becoming a more prominent feature of the work, and, generally speaking, there is a good deal of scope for the exercise of individual initiative and personal responsibility. It is refreshing to note that this fundamentally serious approach to the work operates without undue solemnity on the part of either teachers or taught. An excellent relationship appears to exist between them, largely because they are conscious of working together for a common purpose.

In collaboration with the headmaster, heads of departments have an important part to play in planning the extended courses, in relating them to the work of the school as a whole and in ensuring, through their syllabuses and departmental meetings, that everyone in the school is offered a well-balanced, varied, and appropriate curriculum. The school is fortunate in having a staff who have confronted these problems with a determination to do full justice to the needs of every pupil, with the result that, though differentiated courses of study are provided, the school appears as a unity.

The standard of handwriting is low. Arithmetic, for which no apparatus of any kind is provided, consists of calculation by the mechanical counting of pencil strokes made on paper. No understanding of processes is achieved at any stage; 5-year-olds were found doing sums in tens and units without being able to add one to two, and at least two of the older pupils in the class, aged 7 and 8, could only reduce pence to shillings or shillings to pounds by making the necessary number of strokes and marking them off in twelves and twenties.

In place of a syllabus teachers are expected to teach from the books provided. But the majority of the textbooks used in English, geography, and the elusive subject called general knowledge or general intelligence, are in fact collections of tests, so that nearly all the teaching in these subjects – more than a third of the pupils' time in school – is not teaching at all but the preparation, performance, and correction of tests. The tests themselves are not directed to building up a systematic structure of knowledge; the questions have all the disconnected variety that characterizes the 'quiz' and if they leave any deposit in the minds of the pupils it can only be a jumbled miscellany of relatively unimportant information.

It is worth remembering that the inspectors do not give orders, either to teachers or to the local authorities. Their job is to inspect, to praise or blame, and to advise. It is the job of those in charge of the schools to do whatever seems necessary. Teachers do not necessarily see an H.M.I.'s report. Once it is complete a report may not be altered except by the writer.

Inspectors do more than simply see that schools and teachers are up to standard. They act as the local representatives of the Department and, more important so far as teachers are concerned, are available for advice. Teachers often feel that the inspectors are a little remote from day-to-day problems and rather better at educational theory than practice, but the fault is not only with the inspectors. Few teachers 'use' the inspectorate as intelligently as they might: perhaps they are deterred by the inspectors' 'police' functions. As well as advising by whatever personal contact they may have with the schools, the inspectors also run refresher courses and other short courses for teachers. They also very largely produce the pamphlets and booklets issued by the Department to help teachers and inform the public. A good example of this is the pamphlet issued in 1961 called *Science in Primary Schools* (Department of Education Pamphlet No. 42, H.M.S.O., 15p). The contents of this pamphlet include 'the meaning of science at this (the primary) stage', 'constructing the syllabus', 'how far can a topic be pursued?', and notes on books and apparatus. Inspectors also act as go-betweens between the Department and other educational bodies. They sit on boards and committees and join in less formal discussions as observers. What they see in schools and education offices, the suggestions they hear, the grumbles they overhear, can all be translated into pamphlets, proposals, and action.

Central Advisory Council Reports Apart from the inspectors, who are built-in sources of advice to the Department, the Minister can consult a whole series of people and organizations. He has two bodies imposed on him by law: the two Central Advisory Councils, one for England and the other for Wales. Unlike their predecessor, the Consultative Committee of the Board of Education, the Central Advisory Councils can take the initiative in advising the Minister on educational theory and practice. In practice this privilege has scarcely been used. In recent years the Central Advisory Council for Education (England) has, under the successive chairmanships of Sir Geoffrey Crowther, Mr (later Sir) John Newsom and Lady Plowden, produced three fat reports on large areas of the schools system. These reports are important for several reasons. The first is that they commission and use surveys and inquiries. The Crowther Report, for instance, showed from a survey of national servicemen how far ability, particularly in working class children, was going to waste. A second reason is that they establish and make public what is generally accepted as best educational practice. They are seldom revolutionary documents: instead they stake out the frontiers of acceptable innovation in educational thought and practice. A third reason is that they make possible change by general consent. Not all their recommendations are accepted by Governments, but those that are have had the ground well prepared. This is because the Council's method is to take 'evidence' from every conceivable organization, interest and individual. Much of this evidence is published as it is given, so a climate of opinion gradually builds up which is ready for change.

The Crowther Report, *15 to 18*, was published in 1959 and was on the education of young people between those ages. Its main recommendations were: that the school leaving age should be raised to sixteen between 1966 and 1969; that there should be two leaving dates a year instead of three; that there should be a phased introduction of the county colleges of the 1944 Act; that over-specialization in sixth forms should be combated; an expansion of day-release for vocational training and the development of a coherent national system of practical education; the development of full-time practical education.

Of these recommendations, that on the school leaving age has been accepted, though for a later date: the school leaving age will be raised in 1972–3, not a very practicable year to do it; over-specialization in the sixth may have been slightly mitigated, though competition for university entrance has increased: day-release has not been expanded, despite the Industrial Training Act, and we are still far from the Crowther ideals on practical education. County colleges remain a dead duck.

When it was published, the report was 'accepted in principle' by the Government and then embalmed. This was an interesting example of Ministerial sleight of hand in avoiding taking the advice he himself had asked for. The report argued at length and in detail that the size of classes could be reduced and the school leaving age raised to 16 by 1968–9 if the intention were announced and the plans made at once (that is, in 1959). The Minister pleaded that he could not set such a date for raising the age because his first duty was to reduce the size of classes!

Two aspects of the Crowther Report offer a good measure of recent educational change. The report complained that the proportion of the national income devoted to education was much the same in 1959 as it was before the war. Since then it has grown rapidly. The report's conclusion on comprehensive schools was that the 'only sensible attitude [is] a non-dogmatic one that neither condemns them unheard nor regards them as a prescription of universal application.' Comprehensive reorganization is now well under way.

The Newsom Report, *Half our Future*, was published in 1963 and was on the education, between 13 and 16, of pupils of average or less than average ability. Its main recommendations were: that the school leaving age should be raised to 16 for pupils entering secondary schools from September 1965 onwards; research into social handicaps; an interdepartmental working party on the problems of slums; longer hours, boarding experience, vocationally related courses and higher status for older pupils; internal leaving certificates, but resistance to external examinations;

experimental building programmes and more improvement to existing schools; a training requirement for graduate teachers.

Of these, the one on the school leaving age was accepted (for pupils entering secondary schools in 1966, then postponed for a further two years); most of the others have been intermittently started. It might be argued that the Certificate of Secondary Education meets the Council's fears on external examinations.

The Newsom Report contained a good statistical description of the children it was considering. The introduction, by the then Minister of Education, Sir Edward Boyle, was a landmark. He wrote, 'The essential point is that all children should have an equal opportunity of acquiring intelligence ...' This sentence marked the acceptance of new thinking about intelligence and sounded the death knell of selection at 11 plus.

The Plowden Report, *Children and their Primary Schools*, was published early in 1967. Its title is self-explanatory. Its main recommendations were: there should be more participation by parents in their children's education; educational priority areas should be designated for 'positive discrimination' – more teachers, buildings, books, equipment, research, etc., special efforts for the children of immigrants; more integrated health and social services; ten-year surveys of the effectiveness of primary education; a large expansion of nursery education; a three-year course in the 'first (now infant) school, a four-year course in the 'middle' (now junior) school and transfer to secondary education at 12; recurring national surveys of attainment; the end of corporal punishment; more flexible school organization and the gradual ending of streaming; more teacher's aides.

Of these recommendations educational priority areas are now an established idea. There has been an 'urban programme' of building, including nursery schools, and teachers in E.P.A.s have had extra allowances. Five experimental projects have been undertaken. Some middle schools are emerging in the course of comprehensive reorganization.

The Plowden Report differed from its predecessors in that it began with a chapter called *The Children: Their Growth and Development*. This was the first time one of the Council's reports had started from what is known about child development, and although some of the subsequent recommendations were imperfectly related to the facts and principles set out, this must be regarded as something of a landmark.

The Central Advisory Councils are the only advisory bodies that the Secretary of State is bound to appoint by law, but they have in fact been in abeyance since the Plowden Report and its Welsh counterpart were published. The National Advisory Council on the Training and Supply of Teachers is also in abeyance and the Secondary School Examinations Council (set up in 1917) has disappeared into the Schools Council. The National Advisory Council on Education for Industry and Commerce soldiers on. The Secretary of State can also set up departmental committees to advise him on specific problems. The committee under Lady Albemarle which reported on the youth service in England and Wales in 1960 was one of these. The Ministry of Education and the Scottish Education Department jointly appointed the committee under Sir Colin Anderson to look into grants to university students, and following their report in 1960 a standing advisory committee on grants to students was set up by both departments.

The other people constantly consulted by the Secretary of State include the local authorities, often through their associations, the teachers' organizations, the churches, university departments of education and private individuals.

The Schools Council The Schools Council for Curriculum and Examinations was established in 1964. Its purpose is to do research and development work in curricula, teaching methods and examinations in schools, including the organization of schools so far as this affects curricula. It offers advice on request to schools and others, and publishes reports, articles and pamphlets. Very importantly, in view of initial suspicions of a centralized control of curriculum, it sticks to the principle 'that each school should have the fullest possible measure of responsibility for its own work, with its own curriculum and teaching methods based on the needs of its own pupils and resolved by its own staff.'

The Council has an annual budget of about £1¼m. coming roughly equally from central and local government. It operates through a structure of interlinked committees served by a small secretariat. On all these committees teachers are in a majority. The Programme Committee is responsible for determining policy and priorities: it sets up the inquiries, research and curriculum development projects, publications and so on through which the Council works. Subject committees keep under review each branch of the curriculum, including English, history, geography, science, mathematics, modern languages, art, social science, home economics, physical education, music, classics, religious education, general studies and CAST (craft, applied science and technology).

When founded, the Council took over the work of the Secondary School Examinations Council: now it is responsible for both the General Certificate of Education and the Certificate of Secondary Education. In order to get effective coordination between the two exams and between curriculum and examinations, there are two committees, one for those examinations normally taken at 16-plus, like C.S.E. and G.C.E. O-level, and the other for those taken later, like G.C.E. A-level.

At present the Council has in hand about 100 large and small curriculum development and research projects, and it is associated with a number of projects supported by the Nuffield Foundation. It has published over 20 examinations bulletins, largely on C.S.E. trial examinations; curriculum bulletins, on maths, technology, science and home economics; three dozen working papers including ones on raising the school leaving age, sixth form work and socially disadvantaged children; reports, discussion kits, teaching materials, films and a host of other publications.

LOCAL EDUCATION AUTHORITIES

Under the 1944 Act one of the chief functions of the Secretary of State is to see that local authorities carry out the national policy for providing a varied and comprehensive education service in every area (the word 'comprehensive' is a coincidence: nobody in 1944 thought this meant comprehensive reorganization as it is now taking place). It is almost solely through the local authorities that the state education service is operated. To do this effectively the local authorities in 1944 had to be given powers and duties over the whole of education (except the universities) and to be of reasonable size and financial standing. This meant that authorities which before 1944 had powers for nothing but elementary education had to be abolished, and rather than make educational reform dependent on some future local government reform, councils of counties and of county boroughs were made the local education authorities for their areas.* In order to smooth the transition and to keep such interest as there was in education in the old elementary education authorities, county councils were required to make schemes for partitioning themselves into divisions which would be in some ways responsible for primary and secondary education. The bodies in charge of these divisions are known as divisional executives. Certain municipal boroughs and urban districts could claim to be excepted from their local county's scheme and have the right to prepare, in consultation with the county, their own schemes of divisional administration. In an excepted district the local council is the executive. In other divisions the executive is composed of representatives of such authorities as there are in the division, representatives of the county and co-opted members. Normally, excepted districts have more powers and functions than simple divisional executives, but neither can borrow money nor levy a rate.

It is Section 6 of the Act which says that the local education authority for each county shall be the council of the county and the local education authority for each county borough shall be the council of the county borough, and it goes on to deal with the transfer of property and officers from the old authorities to the new. The duties of the authorities are set out in Section 7. This says that the state system of education shall be organized in three progressive stages – primary, secondary, and further education. It goes on, 'It shall be the duty of the local education authority for every area so far as their powers extend to contribute to the spiritual, moral, mental, and physical development

---

* In 1965, following the reorganization of London government, the new London boroughs became local education authorities, except those in the old London County Council area. There the education authority is a special committee of the Greater London Council: the Inner London Education Authority.

LOCAL EDUCATION AUTHORITIES

of the community by securing that sufficient education throughout those stages shall be available to meet the needs of the population of their area.' This is a tall order, and the Act goes into more detail later. The reorganization implied in the first part of Section 7, and particularly the reorganization of primary and secondary education into separate stages, was begun after the war and is now virtually complete. As if in celebration, the Education Act 1964 allows local authorities to vary the precise age of transfer to secondary school. The second part of Section 7 seems even more sweeping. The duty to contribute towards the 'moral' development of the community is even assumed to imply that the duties of the authorities include giving sex education. Under a much later section (Section 76) the authorities must have regard to the general principle that (with the numerous qualifications discussed at length on pages 140–47) pupils are to be educated in accordance with the wishes of their parents.

Duties and Powers

The duties and powers of a local education authority are very extensive. To take their duties first:

1) They have to see that in their area there are enough schools to give primary and secondary education. Those schools must be of the right size, of the right sorts, and well enough equipped to give all pupils an education offering the variety of instruction and training made desirable by their different ages, abilities, and aptitudes. The authorities must have regard to the need for offering primary and secondary education in separate schools and nursery schools or classes to children under 5, for special training for handicapped children and boarding accommodation for pupils who are considered by their parents and the authority to need it.

2) They have to ensure that the school premises of all their schools conform to the Secretary of State's standards.

3) They must make instruments and articles of management or government for every county primary or secondary school.

4) They must see that in every county school there is a daily

act of worship and regular religious instruction in accordance with an agreed syllabus.

5) They must ascertain what children in their area require special educational treatment.

6) They must see that parents carry out the duties placed on them by the Act to cause their children of compulsory school age to have suitable, efficient, full-time education and to enforce the regular attendance of the children at school.

7) They must make adequate arrangements for further education.

8) When county colleges come to be founded, local authorities must establish and maintain them and enforce the attendance of young persons.

9) They must provide medical inspection and see that medical attention is available free to pupils in their schools.

10) They must provide, in accordance with regulations, 'milk, meals and other refreshments' for pupils in their schools.

11) They are responsible for adequate facilities for recreation and social and physical training in their area.

12) They must suitably cleanse verminous pupils.

13) They must offer, where necessary, free transport for pupils or pay reasonable travelling expenses.

14) They must make provision for the education of children formerly determined as unsuitable for education at an ordinary school.

15) They must carry out directions of the Secretary of State requiring them to establish, maintain, or assist a training college.

16) They must supply the Secretary of State and the Minister of Health with such reports and information as they require.

17) They must appoint a Chief Education Officer.

18) They must keep an account of the monies they get and spend.

Those are the duties of the local education authorities. In addition they have a large number of powers which they may exercise, either subject to the approval of the Secretary of State or in accordance with the regulations.

1) They may establish a new school and maintain as a county

school one that was a voluntary school before 1944, or they may cease to maintain a school.

2) They can group schools under one management.

3) Subject to limitations they can control the use of voluntary schools' premises.

4) They may control secular education in schools.

5) They may normally control the appointment of teachers.

6) They can provide board and lodging for pupils, and if necessary they can provide clothing for pupils.

7) They can make special arrangements for children to be educated otherwise than at school.

8) They can stop the employment of any child, if it is prejudicing his health or otherwise making him unfit to obtain the benefit of his education.

9) They can cause any of their educational establishments to be inspected.

10) They can make arrangements for 'milk, meals and other refreshments' or clothing for pupils at independent schools.

11) They can pay expenses of children at their schools to enable them to take part in school activities, and they can pay the fees or expenses of children at independent schools and grant scholarships or other allowances to pupils over the compulsory school age.

12) They can assist research and organize conferences about education.

13) They can give money to any university or university college.

14) They may accept gifts – for educational purposes.

15) They may compulsorily purchase land required for the purposes of their functions under the Act.

Shapes and Sizes

There are 146 local education authorities in England and 17 in Wales, making 163 in all. These are the councils of 59 administrative counties and of the 83 county boroughs, of the 20 outer London boroughs and the Inner London Education Authority, a committee of the Greater London Council. The Inner London

Education Authority has a population of about 3 million (like Norway) and its annual expenditure on education is about £175m. The county of Rutland has only about 30,000 people in it and spends £1½m. a year on education. The product of a 1d. rate in Bournemouth is £43,000; in Gateshead it is £14,000. The area of the Lancashire authority is 1,600 sq. m. – 11 times that of the Isle of Wight which is 147 sq. m.

Education Committees

The ordinary elected members of county councils and county borough councils need not know anything about education; they are elected to exercise all the responsibilities of local government. For this reason the 1944 Education Act required every local education authority to establish such education committees as were necessary to carry out their functions in education. The arrangements they make for this have to be approved by the Secretary of State. In practice each council appoints one education committee which in turn appoints several sub-committees to deal with particular aspects of education. For example, there are invariably sub-committees for primary, secondary, and further education. Every education committee must include people with experience in education and people acquainted with local education conditions. At least a majority of every education committee must be members of the education authority. The authority themselves must consider a report from the committee before exercising any of their functions in education and may authorize an education committee to exercise any of their functions in education except borrowing money or raising rates. Minutes of education committees are open to inspection by any local elector for a fee of not more than five pence.

There is room for wide variations in the amount of power an authority may delegate to its committee. Some leave almost all decisions to the committee and simply formally approve them in full council. Others expect committees to make recommendations only and these have to await discussion and approval by the council.

Probably most local councils nowadays are elected on party

lines, and the policy of a council and its education committee can change quite drastically with the change of control. For example, after the war Middlesex, with a Labour majority, decided to establish a system of comprehensive schools. In 1949 a Conservative majority reversed this decision. On the other hand, Essex has had a change of political control at almost every election since the war, and this has in itself meant that the political parties have not drastically reversed each other's decisions. As with parliamentary elections, people do not normally vote with education chiefly in mind. They elect councillors to run the whole apparatus of local government and vote as much on national as on local issues. This is slightly less realistic in local than in national elections because education is by far the largest and most important function of local councils: in Parliament its place is more modest.

The people ultimately responsible for education in a county or county borough are the elected local councillors. The chairman of the education committee is bound to be a person of great influence, and the chairmen of sub-committees are also important and influential. Normally, when some educational question comes before the local authority, it is taken to the education committee, who will more than likely refer it to the appropriate sub-committee. When the report of the sub-committee is received the education committee will make a decision and refer it for approval, formal or otherwise, by the council. Anything that involves spending money is discussed with the council's finance committee, because their concurrence is vital. Throughout all these deliberations the council and committee members have the help and advice of salaried officials just as the Minister is assisted by his civil servants.

The permanent paid officers of the local education authority are headed by the chief education officer. He may be called the education officer, director of education, or secretary for education, but whatever he is called he must exist. Under him there is a hierarchy of deputy and assistant education officers, perhaps with special responsibility for particular branches of education. The local education authority may have its own inspectorate (who are not the same as H.M.I.s and who are responsible to the chief education officer). The authority will also normally have people called organizers or county advisers for music, physical education, horticulture, bee-keeping, and so on. Also on the staff of the education authority are the county librarian, the county youth employment officer, the school medical officer, and the dental officer, and perhaps the architect and the treasurer, though these last four officers may be shared with other departments of the council (see page 198).

The range of institutions run by the local education authorities is very impressive. There are, of course, the normal primary and secondary schools. There are also nursery schools and special schools, both day and residential, for handicapped or maladjusted children. A local authority is likely to run a technical college, a college of art, or a farm institute. It will have a whole lot of youth employment bureaux and may well run a teacher-training college. The former colleges of advanced technology are now universities and are being financed through the University Grants Committee, but they were originally founded and supported by the local education authorities. All the new universities founded since the war have been largely supported, until they received their charters, by local authorities. At Brighton, for example, the four local authorities in Sussex gave the site and the working capital to see the project launched.

It is the local authority, too, that decides which kinds of schools there should be, whether infant and junior schools shall be housed in the same building, and whether these schools shall be co-educational or not. It is the local authorities which decide what kinds of secondary schools there shall be and how many of each. This is still true despite secondary reorganization. The shape of secondary education will be even more diverse after reorganization than it was before. The schools, colleges and other institutions run by the local authorities are described in Chapters 4 and 9.

THE AUTHORITIES – AND PARENTS

It is all very well describing the Department of Education and Science and the local authorities, and listing their duties and powers. But education is a personal matter. It succeeds or fails with children not with systems. A parent may be overwhelmed by the special problems of his child and puzzled where to look for help. Authority assumes many varied aspects. When a parent wants something, who is competent to give decisions – or even to advise? Is it the teacher, the chief education officer, the 'committee', or the Department of Education and Science? Often a parent feels that all these are in a conspiracy to make him and his child conform to the pattern they think best. All this is characteristic of modern society. Anyone with an individual need finds himself confronted with our administrative organization of laws, regulations, and officials, all giving, or purporting to give, decisions. How is the parent to know who is really responsible and who should really decide?

The Law

Decisions in education are based ultimately on law, that is, the series of Education Acts from 1944 onwards. Individuals making decisions – whether they are teachers, a clerk in the education office, a chief education officer, an officer of the Department, or even the Secretary of State – express as individuals decisions based on law. Nobody can authorize a procedure that is prohibited by law or refuse a right that is specifically granted by it. For example, full-time education from 5 to 15 years, at school or not, is compulsory. This is an encroachment on the liberty of individual parents and children, but the encroachment is limited by law. No authority from the lowest to the highest can compel a child to receive full-time education before the beginning of term following his fifth birthday, or to remain in full-time education a day longer than a stated time following his fifteenth birthday. To a parent who wants his child to leave early to take a job, the answer is final, whatever the need of the parent, the quality and opportunity of the job or the weakness of the child at school. In this matter, the Secretary of State has no more power than the school, the welfare officer, or the head teacher. They are all bound by the Act. So is the parent, and if he objects there are only two things he can do: the first is to break the law by taking away the child regardless and hoping the local authority will not prosecute; the second is to change the law, by agitation and political action.

A good example of this principle concerns the raising of the compulsory school age. The Secretary of State can raise the age to 16 in 1972 because the 1944 Act provides for it. But establishing two leaving dates a year instead of three while the age remained 15 was illegal – until the 1962 Act.

So if a parent wants an action taken or curbed, a right allowed or an abuse stopped, the first question is, what do the Education Acts say on the point?

The Courts

But an Education Act may be poorly framed or out of date. It may be ambiguous, or various sections of it may have become inconsistent as a result of amendments during its journey through Parliament. It may need interpretation as to what Parliament really meant or as to its relation with the legal principles of society. When there is a clash of opinion the authoritative interpretation is given by the courts. Again, people giving decisions on behalf of authority have to do so within the framework of legal decisions on the subject.

For example, the Education Acts say that the statutory walking distance for a child up to 8 is two miles, and over 8 three miles. Under that distance the authority cannot be compelled to pay bus fares or provide transport. Over that distance, it must. But how do you measure three miles? Is it along a road, across a field, the way the bus goes, from the doorstep, or from the bus stop? Can the authority pay half the fare or merely the part over two or three miles? What happens if there are no pavements or if the traffic is exceptionally dangerous? And supposing one child lives 2.9 miles from a school, his friend lives 3.1 miles but in the same road, and the bus stop is in the middle – what then? Clearly dozens of particular problems arise from the seemingly simple statement, and on all of them the courts have decided. It has been decided, for example, that a route need not be a road, and that distance, not safety, is the test for deciding the nearest available route.

THE COURTS

Another example is a curious one. The law says that compulsory full-time education ends at the school-leaving date following a child's fifteenth birthday. But when does a child reach its fifteenth birthday, and at what time during the day? What about the child who is 15 on the day that term starts? The courts have decided on this. A person attains a given age at the beginning of the day before the anniversary of his birth.

Two particular legal judgements in education have become famous. The first, Watts *v* Kesteven, showed how weak were parents' rights under Section 76 of the 1944 Act. It is fully discussed on page 140. The second is more recent. In the summer of 1967 a group of parents in Enfield took the borough council (the local education authority) to court to try to stop its scheme of secondary reorganization. They claimed that it was illegal as the council had not followed the procedure laid down in Section 13 of the 1944 Act in respect of eight schools. This procedure provides for the publication of notices and the possibility of objection if an authority proposes to establish or cease to maintain a school. The judgement turned on whether the local authority, in turning a grammar school and a secondary modern school into a senior and junior comprehensive school respectively, was in effect ceasing to maintain two schools and establishing two others. The judge said they would be doing so if they were making a change in the fundamental character of the school – but what constituted such a change? Merely changing a grammar or secondary modern school into a comprehensive school, he said, was not in itself changing the fundamental character – but changing the age range (admitting pupils at 14 instead of 11) or taking in pupils of a different sex was. The judgement is remote from educational experience and common sense, but the Education Act, 1968, was passed to accommodate it.

On these and similar points the Secretary of State and the authorities, and the officers who act for them, are bound by the decisions of the courts. Only Parliament can make the law – and only the courts can determine what it is.

The Secretary of State

Another source of decisions arises from the Secretary of State's power to make regulations. These have been described on page 42. Once made, regulations have the force of law, though the Secretary of State can make regulations only where he is given specific power to do so by Act of Parliament. The Education Act, 1944, says a child between 5 and 15 years must have full-time education, but 'full-time' has been defined by the Secretary of State in the Schools Regulations. On a whole series of educational matters the Secretary of State has issued regulations which are binding on authorities and officers. So after a parent has discovered in a particular case what the Education Acts say about it and what legal judgements have been given, his third question is, has the matter been covered by the Secretary of State's regulations?

The Local Authority

Formidable as all this is, it still leaves a lot to local discretion. No local education authority can violate Acts of Parliament or act contrary to legal judgements or the Secretary of State's regulations, but there are opportunities for local variations. Some local authorities find it necessary to impose local uniformity. Holidays are a good example. The 1944 Act says that pupils of compulsory school age should have full-time education. The Schools Regulations say this means that a school shall be open on a minimum of 400 sessions (200 days) of the year. The authority regulates the main dates of the holidays but often leaves to local governors or managers, or to the schools themselves, the dates of half terms and other minor holidays.

Again, the 1944 Act says that education for pupils over 12 shall be secondary (as distinguished from primary) in character. The decision about what kinds of schools there shall be (grammar, secondary modern, or comprehensive, for example) and which particular kind of school a pupil shall attend is a matter for the local authority. Even with secondary reorganization under way, this is still so. The actual course of instruction, the curriculum and organization of the school, is a matter for the headmaster and his staff. If a parent wants a council to do something involving a new decision or spending money, the people to go for are the councillors themselves, the elected or co-opted members of the education committee and, where appropriate, of the finance committee. If a parent doesn't like what they decide, all he can do is try to change them at the next election. If a local education authority does something within its discretion that a parent objects to, the parent's only redress is to persuade the authority to change their minds – or to undertake political action to change the composition of the county council and through this of the education committee. It is possible to appeal to the Secretary of State under Section 68 of the 1944 Act that the local education authority are acting unreasonably, but in practice the Secretary of State rarely overrules the authority. A recurrent example of this is that authorities sometimes wish to change a co-educational school into two single-sex schools or vice versa. If parents object to this, their remedy has always to be through local campaigns to change either the minds or the actual composition of the education committee. Parents who have appealed to the Secretary of State have normally found that he will not act.

If a parent wants something done within the context of decisions already taken by the education committee, he should go and have a word with an officer at the local education office. If he wants some special treatment or consideration, or if he feels he has been hardly dealt with, his remedy is through his elected representative. Although the chief education officer and his staff may influence greatly the decisions of the committee (in some areas there are whispers of dictation by the chief officer) the decisions are those of the committee and the officer can only act consistently with them.

The School

Traditionally in Britain, the courses of instruction offered in a school, its organization, ethos, and curriculum, are matters for the head teacher and staff. If a primary school headmistress insists that a child wait a term or a year before going up from the infant to the junior department, or if a secondary school headmaster cannot or will not allow a child to take a particular subject, there is little a parent can do about it. He can appeal to the education officer, but is likely to be told that what goes on in schools is the responsibility of the head. He can appeal to the governors, but they are not likely to make the head change. All the parent can do is try to persuade the head to change his mind. Failing that, he can remove his child to another school, if this is possible.

CHAPTER FOUR

The Schools

ALL schools in England and Wales are to some extent governed by Act of Parliament. It is, for example, illegal to run a school that is not registered with the Department of Education and Science and registration may be refused if the school is not good enough. But one distinction can be made at once, between the 30,000 state schools and 3,000 independent schools. There are several kinds of schools in each of these groups, and the purpose of this chapter is to describe them, starting in each case from schools for the very youngest children and working up. It may be as well to show at the beginning that a child's journey through state and independent schools proceeds in similar though not identical stages.

STATE		INDEPENDENT	
Age	*Type of School*	*Age*	*Type of School*
2–5	nursery	2–5	nursery
5–7	infant } primary	5–8	pre-preparatory
7–11	junior }	8–13	preparatory
11–18	secondary (secondary modern, grammar, comprehensive, etc.)	13–18	public, direct grant, etc.

Hitherto half the children in state schools have left at the school leaving age. Very few in independent schools do so. A few local authorities are taking advantage of the 1964 Act to set up 'middle schools' for pupils aged 9 to 13 or 9 to 14. Independent schools for younger children very often will not fit into precise categories and the change to secondary schools for girls often takes place at 11 in independent as in state schools.

Before describing different kinds of schools, it may be as well to discuss those things which most schools have in common.

1) SCHOOL ORGANIZATION

The basic organization of most schools is chronological. In a way this is forced on them by the Education Act. Children must be more or less the same age when they start at a primary school, when they transfer from primary to secondary school, and when they leave. Whatever combinations or groupings may be devised, most children go through their school lives in company with their strict contemporaries. Thus the children entering secondary school go into the first form, move on together at the end of the year to the second form, and so on up to the fifth or sixth form. The syllabuses they follow are normally arranged to be self-contained within a year. The exceptions to this are in the infant school, where children may 'go up' from one class to another more than once a year, and in the sixth forms of grammar schools, where the work is normally planned over two years. As usual in education nomenclature varies considerably but in secondary schools at any rate an age group (say 12- to 13-year-olds) is known as a form or year.

If 100 children enter a school at the age of 11 they can clearly not be taught as one group and they are thus split up into smaller groups. These smaller groups, with say thirty children in each, are called classes (or, to confuse the issue, forms). However much a class may move around or be split up for particular subjects, it will normally have a class teacher and a classroom in which it keeps its books and things. As a general rule a class will stay with one teacher very much more in the primary than in the secondary school.

In secondary schools there are all kinds of exotic groupings imposed on the straightforward class system. The children may be grouped according to their ability for specific subjects and the divisions will perhaps be called 'sets'. A year with three classes may even be sub-divided, for modern languages, say, into four sets. Setting is also possible where the children have a choice of subjects. A fourth form of three classes may divide into three quite different sets, two doing geography and one doing biology.

Perhaps an example will make this clear. A child of 13 may be in the third form of his grammar school. The class with whom he is normally taught may be class 3A. The form may be divided into four sets for mathematics and our boy may be in set 3/2 or 3/3. There may be a choice between woodwork and German and our boy may choose to be in the only woodwork set rather than one of the two German sets.

Where basic class divisions in any one form or year are made according to ability, this is known as streaming. The most able children are in the A stream, the least able in the D, E, or perhaps even the L stream. Sometimes the existence of streaming is disguised by giving the classes the initial letters of their teachers' names rather than A, B, or C. In posh grammar schools they may add a touch of colour by calling the streams alpha, beta, and gamma. Streaming can start as early as the infant school, and when it happens here it often leads to a great deal of criticism from parents. It need hardly be added that when in secondary schools the classes are themselves streams the whole apparatus of setting and subdivision can still be superimposed.

School 'Houses'

Most schools have some kind of 'house' system. As the name implies, this derives from the practice of boarding schools. Boys or girls there actually live in different houses, and house spirit and inter-house rivalry emerge naturally. In day schools 'houses' can be somewhat artificial creations – though a lot of big schools are turning to some sort of house system as a way of making certain that the children have some member of the staff as well as a class teacher or subject teachers to turn to and rely on. In a boarding school the role of the house master is an obvious one – he stands very much *in loco parentis*. A day school house master may have the same function but he will in the nature of things see much less of the pupil and will not need to exercise so much semi-parental responsibility. The most obvious demonstration of a house system and the house feeling in day schools is the school sports day, though there may be all kinds of other house rivalries, in team games, play competitions, and so on. The houses can also be used as a way of giving more pupils responsibility. There can be only one school captain. There may be four house captains. A class has one form captain but many have four form house captains.

A faint echo of the house system is also prevalent in primary schools. The 'houses' tend to have homely names like blues, greens, and reds, or robins, eagles, and swifts, and their chief function may be disciplinary. Every week the good and bad conduct points gained by members of the houses in their normal class work and play may be read out in school assembly. The 'houses' may also be the basis for *ad hoc* rivalries in physical education lessons.

Prefects

Another practice which has spread from boarding schools into day schools is that of appointing senior pupils to hold authority. In practice this normally means helping to keep discipline at times when the school comes together or is moving about. In boarding schools the house captain may exercise all but the most extreme disciplinary powers of the house master. The head of the school in boarding schools is a really splendid figure. In day schools there is less for the prefects to do but they are expected to contribute to the 'tone' of the place, stop people running in corridors, and try and impose some kind of table manners at lunch time. They may also have some administrative duties, like organizing school prayers. Secondary modern schools have often imitated the system – with better results in some than in others.

Teachers

There are two main ways in which people become teachers. They either take a three-year course in a college of education or get a university degree. In the past graduates could teach without further training, but from 1971 in primary schools and 1974 in secondary schools new graduates will need a year's training before they can be recognized by the D.E.S. as qualified teachers. One fifth of the teachers in state schools are graduates. Of the graduates, nearly 45,000 have been trained as teachers and over 19,000 are untrained. There are 3,000 non-qualified teachers in a total teaching force of some 313,000.

The qualifications for entering a college of education are somewhat lower than those needed for going to university, but they are by no means as low as they appear on paper. The minimum entrance requirement for a college of education is five passes at G.C.E. O level. In fact only 10 per cent of all the candidates going into colleges of education in 1970 had only the minimum qualifications and probably very many of these had taken some form of sixth-form course at school. Increasingly the colleges are demanding two A levels for entry. Over a third of entrants in 1970 had two or more A levels – and two A levels are the minimum requirement for universities.

There are two main kinds of college of education: the general college and the specialist college. The specialist colleges concentrate on training teachers for particular subjects like housecraft (now called home economics), physical education, handicraft (woodwork and metalwork), music, drama, or arts and crafts.

In the general colleges a teacher's training is made up of four interrelated elements. First there is the student's own personal education. Colleges differ, but in most of them a student chooses one or two subjects and takes them to as high an academic level as he can. He starts at A level and probably reaches something like the standard of a pass degree. Second, training college students study 'education'. They study children and young people as they grow up – how they think, how they feel and how they learn. They also study society and the underlying ideas about the education of children in it. This part of the course includes a certain amount of history, philosophy, psychology, and sociology. Third, the students learn about teaching methods and the theoretical basis of teaching particular skills and subjects. Fourth, a large part of the course is taken up with practical work in schools. Students first observe children in classrooms, in playgrounds, and in recreation centres. Gradually they get the chance to take lessons of their own and get continuing practice in doing it. They may do some experimental or research work under the guidance of their college supervisor. And they are likely to be introduced to all kinds of schools – not only primary and different kinds of secondary schools, but also special schools for the handicapped. Since 1963 most teachers in training have done a three-year course.

The year's training for graduates resembles the teacher training course in all its essentials except that the personal education of a student in his specialist subject is taken pretty well for granted. By and large, graduate teachers find themselves teaching in state and independent grammar schools, non-graduate teachers in secondary modern and primary schools. (For the latest proposals on teacher training, see page 194.)

Teachers' Quota Scheme

In the general shortage of teachers, some local authorities have been worse off than others. Genial resorts on the south coast have naturally found it easier to find teachers than depressing slums in the industrial north. The quota scheme is an attempt to distribute teachers more equitably over the country as a whole. Each local authority is notified of the maximum number of teachers of all kinds which it may employ each year, and the hope is that, when a salubrious authority is full up, teachers will look elsewhere for jobs. Part-time teachers and married women who return to teaching are not covered by the quota system.

Teachers' Salaries

In 1919 a committee to deal with teachers' salaries was set up under the independent chairmanship of Lord Burnham. Under the 1944 Act the successor of this first committee gained statutory recognition. The committees which negotiate teachers' salaries are still known as Burnham committees and their recommendations are known as Burnham awards. The committee for primary and secondary school teachers is known as the Burnham Main Committee, and there are other committees for teachers in further education, colleges of education (the Pelham Committee) and farm institutes, and for inspectors, organizers and advisory officers, youth leaders and community centre wardens.

Until 1965 the Burnham Committee consisted of representatives of the teachers' and local authorities' associations only. The Minister of Education had no representatives, and he could approve or reject a Burnham settlement, but not modify one. This worked reasonably well until 1960, when the Minister withheld his approval of a settlement, in accordance with the Government's economic policy. On this occasion the Burnham Committee modified its proposals so that they were acceptable to the Minister. In 1963 the Minister refused to accept the proposed salary scales, largely because he wanted to increase the differentials. This time the committee would not budge, and a special Act of Parliament, the Remuneration of Teachers Act, 1963, had to be passed so that new salary scales could be paid – in accordance with the Minister's wishes. The Act was only an interim measure. The Remuneration of Teachers Act, 1965, repealed both it and Section 89 of the 1944 Act and provided for the setting up of new committees, under an independent chairman as before. The chief innovations of the Act were: the inclusion of representatives of the Secretary of State on the committees; the provision for independent arbitration in case of deadlock; and the provision for an award to be retrospective. In 1971, the negotiations were deadlocked, and there was an arbitrated award of an overall increase of 11 per cent. The chairman of the Burnham Main Committee is Mr J. S. Wordie, and the committee consists of two panels with twenty-eight members each. The management panel consists of nine representatives from the County Councils Association, six each from the Association of Municipal Corporations and the Association of Education Committees, three from the Inner London Education Authority and two each from the Welsh Joint Education Committee and the Department of Education and Science. The influence of the latter is out of proportion to their numbers. The teachers' panel comprises sixteen representatives from the National Union of Teachers (a clear majority), two from the Association of Teachers in Technical Institutions (because the further education negotiations follow and depend on the main ones), three from the National Association of Schoolmasters, two each from the Incorporated Association of Assistant Masters and the Incorporated Association of Assistant Mistresses, and one each from the

Incorporated Association of Headmasters, the Incorporated Association of Headmistresses and the National Association of Head Teachers.

The salary scales themselves are complicated, but a teachers' salary depends on whether or not he is recognized as qualified, the length of his training, whether he has a 'good' honours degree or another sort and whether he teaches in London or not. On top of these basic scales there are further allowances which are made to teachers with special responsibilities. For example, a careers master may get an allowance: so might a teacher in charge of a subject in a secondary school or one working in a special school or, more recently, in an educational priority area. Head teachers get allowances depending on the numbers on the school roll, with a special weighting for older pupils. A deputy head gets a smaller allowance assessed in the same way.

The teachers' superannuation scheme is administered centrally by the Department of Education and Science. It is a contributory and unfunded scheme. Teachers contribute at the rate of 6 per cent and employing authorities 8 per cent, and this is paid into the Exchequer, which bears the charge for pensions, gratuities, and refunded contributions. The benefits payable include annual pensions on retirement and a lump-sum allowance, ill-health awards, and death gratuities. A widows' and orphans' scheme became available for serving teachers in 1966 and is compulsory for new entrants to teaching from April 1969. A separate, optional, scheme for other dependants was introduced also in 1966.

Independent schools are not bound by Burnham awards and are not covered by the superannuation scheme. In order to compete for staff, however, they have to offer Burnham scales – or more. Burnham increases are normally followed, or shrewdly preceded, by increases for those in independent schools.

Hierarchy and Freedom

To an outsider the most obvious thing about English school organization is its hierarchial nature. The head is a (perhaps benevolent) despot, whose sway is tempered, if at all, only by interference from outside or intransigence from the staff.

Normally what he says goes. Among the staff the house masters of boarding schools have their own domains. In day schools the senior subject teachers or heads of departments to some extent control the subjects and staff in their charge. The ordinary teacher is normally a law unto himself in his own classroom. The pupils are similarly arranged. The head boy or head girl leads a team of prefects or monitors, and they are all appointed either by the head or by the staff of the school. House masters appoint house captains and they in turn choose the people below them. There are very few teachers in England who can imagine schools organized in any way different from this. One example will do to point this hierarchial system: the staff of a school normally has no say whatever in the appointment of a new head.

This has big implications for freedom and the exercise of responsibility. Head teachers in particular are probably freer here than anywhere else in the world from outside pressures of any kind, be they from the authorities or from parents. There is a similar tradition of absolute freedom for teachers inside their own classrooms. What is more, an enormous number of the things done in the school – the out-of-school activities, the sports – are very often run, at any rate in secondary schools, by the pupils. Even in primary school selected pupils may be responsible for the arranging of flowers in the hall and standing on sentry-go as the school marches in from the playground.

II) KINDS OF SCHOOLS

STATE SCHOOLS

It may be as well to deal with terminology first. Officially, state schools are called 'maintained schools' or 'grant-aided schools'. As the second of these terms is extremely confusing this is the last time it will appear in this book. A maintained school is one in which the teachers are paid, the general cost of running the school borne, and the inside of the school building 'maintained' by the local education authority. As explained in the preface, 'state schools' is simpler and more readily understandable.

County and Voluntary Schools

State schools are of two kinds, county and voluntary. County schools are provided by the local authority and maintained by them inside and out.

Voluntary schools are those which were initially built by the denominations. Their present status is the result of the compromises made in the 1944 Act in order to create a more uniform system. There are three sorts of voluntary schools: controlled, aided, and special agreement. In a controlled school the local authority is responsible for maintenance inside and out. It appoints two-thirds of the managers or governors and also appoints the teachers, but the managers or governors must be consulted over the appointment of the head teacher and of any teacher giving denominational instruction. Most controlled schools are Church of England schools.

In aided schools it is the governors or managers who maintain the outside of the school building and make enlargements or alterations to it. Religious instruction is controlled by the governors or managers, and the governors of secondary schools control secular as well as religious instruction. The authority, however, has to be satisfied about the qualifications of teachers giving secular instruction. The voluntary body itself is responsible for appointing two-thirds of the managers or governors. If the managers or governors do alter, enlarge, or improve the buildings they may get a grant of up to 80 per cent of the cost. This grant comes direct from the Ministry after approval there and it does not go through the local authorities, though these are consulted. Nearly three-fifths of the aided schools are Church of England schools. All but two Roman Catholic schools are aided, or special agreement.

Special-agreement schools are a hangover from the Education Act of 1936. Local authorities may by special agreement pay between a half and three-quarters of the cost of building a voluntary secondary school. Two-thirds of the governors are appointed by the voluntary body and the rest by the education authority. Maintenance of the school is divided between the local authority and the voluntary body, as in an aided school. The governors control religious instruction and normally have to be consulted over the appointment of teachers giving denominational instruction. The local authority appoints the other teachers.

The numbers of state schools, their pupils and teachers are set out in the table below taken from the Department of Education's *Statistics of Education 1969*, Vol. 1, H.M.S.O. £1.70.

STATE SCHOOLS
January 1969

Kinds of Schools	Numbers of schools or departments	Numbers of pupils	Numbers of full-time teachers
Primary			
Nursery	470	17,170	1,223
Infants	5,549	1,114,448	37,143
Junior with infants	12,543	2,159,369	74,422
Junior without infants	4,949	1,509,227	49,458
All-age	22	5,547	226
Secondary			
Modern	2,954	1,303,751	63,606
Grammar	1,098	631,948	35,370
Technical	109	56,627	3,194
Comprehensive	962	772,612	39,759
Other secondary	331	194,723	9,689
Total	28,987	7,765,422	314,090

The following table lists the state schools except nursery, special, and special hospital schools according to whether they are county or voluntary.

STATE SCHOOLS
COUNTY AND VOLUNTARY SCHOOLS
1969

	Primary	Middle	Secondary	Total
County	14,580	14	4,468	19,062
Voluntary (total) *including:*	8,474	1	986	9,461
Aided .... C. of E.	2,634	1	114	2,749
R.C.	1,940	—	410	2,350
Other	43	—	86	129
Controlled C. of E.	3,737	—	70	3,807
R.C.	1	—	—	1
Other	116	—	153	269
Special-agreement				
C. of E.	2	—	30	32
R.C.	1	—	122	123
Other	—	—	1	1
Not determined				
C. of E.	—	—	—	—

Religious Instruction

It has already been noted that there is one curious exception to the general rule that the curriculum and syllabuses of the schools are matters only for the head teacher and staff. Section 25 of the 1944 Education Act says: 'The school day in every county school and every voluntary school shall begin with collective worship ...' and 'religious instruction shall be given in every county school and every voluntary school.' There are fairly elaborate arrangements for parents to withdraw their children both from the act of worship and the religious instruction if they want to, but every school is compelled by law to provide both unless it can be shown to be physically impossible. In county and controlled schools religious instruction has to be in accordance with an agreed syllabus drawn up by representatives of the religious denominations, the teachers, and the local authority, though in controlled schools there are provisions allowing parents to insist that their children receive instruction in the original denomination of the school. In aided and special-agreement schools the religious instruction has to be in accordance with the original trust deed.

The provisions in the Act about religious worship and instruction are so eccentric and so against the normal practice of allowing teachers freedom as to what they teach that they can only be explained as part of the elaborate bargaining of 1944. In order that children should be properly educated the denominational schools had to be brought up to standard. The only way of doing this was by government action. Government action meant increased government control, and the Government had to offer something in return. What was more, many nonconformists, for example, objected to Anglican indoctrination being financed from the rates they paid; hence the controlled schools. The result of the consequent horse-trading fixed the anomalous religious provisions in the 1944 Act and the agreed syllabuses on the schools of England and Wales.

Managers and Governors

All state schools have to have a body of managers or governors. Primary schools have managers, and secondary schools governors. The object of this is to see that every school can have an individual life of its own as well as a place in the local system. Under the 1944 Act aided schools retained a large measure of independence and it was thought desirable that other state schools should have reasonable autonomy. Managers and governors are appointed under instruments of management or government made for county schools by the local education authority and for voluntary schools by order of the Secretary of State. The instruments vary according to the history, tradition and circumstances of individual schools. In schools other than aided schools, the local authority appoints either all or two-thirds of the governors or managers; the other one-third might be representatives of minor authorities or, in the case of controlled schools, a third might be foundation governors. In aided schools one-third of the governors are appointed by the education authority, and two-thirds are foundation governors. The governors and managers must meet at least once every school term and the local education authority may inspect the minutes of their meetings.

The 1944 Act did allow for several schools to be grouped under one body of managers. This seems to go against the idea that every school should have an individual life and corporate feeling of its own. Schools are normally grouped either when the local education authority has difficulty in finding people sufficiently able and willing to be governors and managers or when it has plans for grouping schools together eventually as a comprehensive school.

People often ask what managers and governors do, and well they might. The rules of management of a primary school are made by the local education authority, and the managers therefore have only such powers (except those mentioned in the Act) as the authority feels like giving them. The articles of government of secondary schools, however, must be approved by the Secretary of State, and in voluntary secondary schools they must be made by him. The articles must determine the functions to be exercised by the local authority, the governors and the head teacher. The then Minister of Education gave guidance in drawing up articles in a White Paper called *Principles of Government in Maintained Secondary Schools* (Cmd 6523). There it was suggested that the governors and the authority should be associated in appointing a head teacher, either by a joint committee consisting of equal numbers of governors and authority representatives or by the authority from a short list drawn up by the governors. The appointment of assistants, it was suggested, should be by the governors in consultation with the head, subject to confirmation by the authority. As for internal organization and the curriculum, the authority would settle the general educational character of the school and its place in the local system, and the governors would have the general direction of the school and the curriculum, while the head would control the internal organization, management, and discipline of the staff. In practice the governors do not interfere with the curriculum. The responsibility for deciding what kind of secondary education an individual child should follow remained with the local education authority too. It was suggested that the governors and the head should play a part in the selection of pupils for their particular school. Disputes should be settled by the Secretary of State. Within limits the managers and governors of aided and special-agreement schools control admissions; this power is regarded as crucial by the denominations in preserving parental choice.

Practice can and does vary from one school to another and from one area to another, but governors of secondary schools are normally active only when staff are appointed and when the dates of minor holidays have to be decided. Children and their parents get a fairly accurate picture of the governors' position from school speech day. At some point the visiting speaker asks the governors to grant an extra half-holiday. The chairman says that he has consulted the governors (when normally he has patently failed to do anything of the kind) and is happy to announce that the request has been granted. The very strong tradition that what goes on at a school is the business of the head teacher normally ensures that the governors have next to no influence on it. Even in the appointment of staff, where they might be supposed to have some say, it is in practice very rare for the governors to do anything but follow a lead given by the headmaster. So far as powers are concerned, they inhabit a kind of no-man's land between the local authority and the head of the school.

It is a mistake, however, to assume that there is no point at all in having governors and managers. If they are active and interested they can help a school create an individual life of its own. Many of them are members of the local authority or are well known to someone who is, so there is some chance that decisions will be made about a school on the basis of at least some personal knowledge or contact. And if it comes to a dispute the governors or managers are a ready-made lobby. They can, and often have, formed the basis of an action comittee to campaign, petition and appeal. Normally, however, the governors turn up at school functions, try to remember the names of the teachers, occasionally badger the authority for improvements to the school premises and hold themselves available for consultation and discussion with the headmaster. In 1970 the National Association of Governors and Managers (N.A.G.M.) was founded to help governors and managers to be more effective and to press for changes in their recruitment and powers.

Nursery Schools

At the beginning of the term after a child's fifth birthday, his parent is compelled by law to see that he receives full-time education. In practice this means that the children are compelled to go to school. There are many parents who think 5 is too young to start school, but there are many more who want their children to go to school before 5 – at $2\frac{1}{2}$, say, or 3. The most obvious reasons for wanting this are physical ones. A child who lives in a town flat or a city street needs somewhere to spend the day, or part of it, where he can run about and play in safety with someone keeping an eye on him. A parent who is widowed, divorced, or unmarried and who has to be out at work will need someone to look after the children. Even mothers who are at home all day can do with a rest from children. Some children are ready for school much earlier than others: they do not wait for administrative convenience or even Acts of Parliament. They may be sociable and enjoy being with large groups of other children for much of the day. Others may need a gentle introduction to the rigours of full-time school, perhaps mornings or afternoons only.

Advocates of nursery schools go farther. They say that in small, isolated families a child does not get the chance to build up enough relationships either with other children of about his own age or with a number of adults. Few single homes can be as rich in variety of experience as a good nursery school, physically, emotionally and educationally. In any case, the best nursery schools are the 'balanced' ones: schools which are not restricted to those cases where need of various kinds is the chief criterion for admission.

When a mother starts looking for a nursery school, she might be confused by the existence of both nursery schools and day nurseries. Broadly speaking, the difference is in the word 'school'. A day nursery meets a social need: it minds children while their parents are at work, and there may be over 75,000 children in this service. A nursery school is an educational establishment and is more positively concerned with the children's development. Nursery schools also operate during the normal school hours and observe normal school holidays. Day nurseries are normally open for longer and remain open virtually all the year round. What is more, you pay according to your income for day nurseries run by the local health authority: the local education authority's nursery schools are free.

This book is principally concerned with education and will concentrate on nursery schools. The most obvious fact about them is that there are not enough. There are 470 or so run by the local education authorities, taking 32,000 children under 5. There are also over 469,000 children under 5 in ordinary primary schools, but most of these are in fact over 4: over 55,000 of them are in nursery classes. As there are two and a half million children of nursery school age, the 87,000 places in local authority nursery classes mean that only about three children in 100 can go to them. This situation is likely to continue because a Minister of Education reaffirmed (in Circular 8 of 1960) an earlier decision that the local authorities must not provide for more nursery school children than at present. Recently this ban has been eased – where the provision of a nursery school would free married women for teaching in the normal schools. Since 1968 an 'urban programme' of over £20m. has been granted to deprived urban areas, partly to provide nursery schools and classes.

As well as the local authority schools there are fifteen direct grant nursery schools, eleven independent nursery schools recognized as efficient by the Department of Education and Science and a number of recognized independent schools which have nursery departments. There are also over 200 unrecognized independent nursery schools and unrecognized schools with nursery departments. There are many small play-groups in halls or private homes which may be unknown to the education authorities because they do not count as schools. The Pre-school Playgroups Association, formed to encourage mothers to establish playgroups for themselves, now has well over 5,000 playgroups associated with it, accommodating over 150,000 children. Not only are there too few nursery schools but those that do exist are very unevenly spread. A parent might find that there is some choice near by: he is more likely to discover that there is only one possibility, and probably most people do not have a nursery school of any kind for miles.

Nursery schools run by the local education authorities and the few independent nursery schools recognized as efficient are staffed by certificated teachers with special training in nursery school work, assistants with the certificate of the National Nursery Examination Board and, quite frequently, by students in training. A nursery class in a primary school should have one teacher and one full-time assistant to thirty children. In a separate nursery school the regulations say there must be one teacher and one full-time assistant for every twenty full-time children: and in nursery schools (unlike other schools) the limitation on the size of classes is strictly enforced.

A nursery school will have space where play can be uninhibited indoors and out. The children spend a lot of time playing on the floor. In summer they move easily from the classroom to the open air, using water, sand, modelling clay, books, toys, climbing frames, planks of wood, and perhaps old car tyres and battered boxes. At times the teachers tell them stories or read to them and there will probably be some singing round a piano or listening to a gramophone. Many children go to nursery schools for only part of the day, either mornings or afternoons. Those who go full-time normally have lunch at school and have a rest period afterwards. This is why nursery schools have low canvas rest beds and coloured blankets. Nursery schools normally take a great deal of trouble to introduce the children to school carefully. Their methods vary; some teachers believe in gradual weaning, others insist the child will be all right when mother has gone. Some teachers believe that it may take weeks before children feel secure enough to be left alone. Others prefer the child to attend regularly and alone but perhaps only once or twice a week at first.

Primary Schools

The first of the three stages of education laid down in the 1944 Act is called the primary stage. The Act says that local education authorities must offer full-time education suitable for junior pupils – which means children under 12. The Act seems to imply that this duty to children starts from the day they are born. They have the more explicit duty, from which they are at present relieved by Circular 8/60, to provide nursery schools for children of 2 and over. The compulsory school age begins at 5 and the authorities must provide enough primary schools for all the children over that age in their area.

Most children, therefore, start school at 5 in a primary school and go on at 11 or 12 to the next stage of education in a secondary school of some kind. A primary school may be divided into two parts – infants and juniors. These may be in separate buildings and have separate head teachers, but they are normally very close together or are housed in the same building under one head. Over 12,000 of the primary schools are junior-with-infants schools. There are 5,500 separate infant schools and 4,900 junior schools, each with its own head. In 1969 there were four and three-quarter million children in primary schools with over 160,000 full-time teachers, under 5 per cent of whom were graduates. Primary schools are normally quite small; most of the infant schools, for example, have between 100 and 300 pupils, and most of the junior schools have between 100 and 400. There is much more variation in the size of the junior-with-infant schools; 700 of them, for example, have under 25 pupils. The great majority of them have under 200. Almost all primary schools are mixed schools. In fact, of over 23,000 primary schools only 182 are for boys alone and 188 for girls alone.

The most obvious fact about state primary schools is that the classes are enormous. In January 1969 twice as many children were in classes of over 30 as there were in classes of under 30. There were nearly 14,000 classes of between 41 and 50 pupils and a few – 91 in fact – with 51 pupils and over. The Schools Regulations used to say that 40 should be the maximum size of a primary school class, but over England and Wales as a whole about 10 per cent of primary classes are oversize by this standard. About one in eight of primary school children are in oversize classes, the average number per teacher is 27·7 and the average size of class is 32·7.

Infant Schools

What goes on in British infant schools has been called 'probably the world's most ambitious pattern of beginning instruction'.*
The methods, to outward view, may seem like an extension of those used in nursery schools. The classroom is normally free and probably noisy. The children are likely to be in groups doing quite different things. Some may be keeping shop, selling each other goods, and keeping accounts; some may be engaged on a 'project', like making a model village. Others will be in a cluster reading together. Even when the whole class is doing more or less the same thing, they are likely to be doing it, not as a body, but in smaller groups. Parents who think of classrooms in terms of rows of desks are often surprised to find that in infant schools the desks are rarely, if ever, in rows. They may be grouped together in squares or placed around the walls. They are often moved about or used as a platform for a class playlet or dispensed with altogether. The infant teachers do what they can, in short, to counteract the effect of large classes. They keep the children in smaller units and offer to each group in turn and to children in it the individual attention that would be impossible if the class were treated as a whole. It is assumed that by the time children are ready for the junior school they will be able to read and write and do simple addition and subtraction of numbers. Between two-thirds and three-quarters of them actually do this.

* Martin Mayer, *The Schools*, Bodley Head, 1961.

PRIMARY SCHOOLS

Junior Schools

At seven or so, children go on from the 'infants' to the junior school. The junior school has the same kind of staff, the same size of classes, and basically the same approach as the infant school. Parents often feel that the transition from the 'infants' to the 'juniors', even more than starting school at 5, marks the transition from play to 'real work'. In many schools this difference is not stark. In most, however, the basic attitudes and methods of the primary school become overlaid with more 'academic' preoccupations when the children pass the age of 7. The selection procedure at 11 casts its shadow forward. 'Streaming' begins (see pages 171–2). The children are consciously graded and teachers begin to have conscious or unconscious expectations of each grade as a whole. The change is subtle and difficult to pin down, but it is in the junior school that teachers normally begin to set standards and judge the children by their success in measuring up to them. Rigidity about the age of transfer from one class to another often starts here too. A date is chosen and all children of a particular age on that date 'go up' to the next class. In many areas the child who is one or two days too young may be 'kept down' although he is physically and mentally advanced.

The curriculum in the junior school begins to be arranged more formally into individual subjects. What was for the infant teacher a rough guide to the sequence of the day's variety becomes in the junior school much more like a time-table. The children have set periods of arithmetic, reading, and composition, which are all 11+ 'subjects'. As they approach the examination, they may be given 'practice' (not, of course, 'coaching') in doing intelligence tests. They will do other subjects too: nature-study, history, geography, singing, drama, physical education, religious knowledge and so on.

Middle Schools

Since the Education Act, 1964, local authorities have been allowed to vary the age of transfer from primary to secondary school. The intention was 'to permit a relatively small number of limited experiments in educational organization.' In 1967 the Plowden Report recommended a change in the age of transfer from 11 to 12 (though their arguments for 13 were almost as strong) and that junior schools should be re-named middle schools. Since then, a number of authorities have suggested middle schools for pupils aged 8 to 12, or 9 to 13, as part of their proposals for secondary reorganization. Only about twenty such schools exist at present.

All-Age Schools

Despite the fact that in 1944 it was determined that primary and secondary schools should be in separate buildings there were still in 1969 22 unreorganized all-age schools taking children for the whole of the compulsory school age from 5 to 15. There are 5,500 children in them and 640 teachers. Nearly all of the 22 are denominational schools. But all-age schools ought to have disappeared in a year or two.

Secondary Schools

Reorganization

The second stage of education laid down in the 1944 Act is the secondary stage. At present, it is being reorganized on 'comprehensive' lines, and will be for many years to come. In some sense this is an attempt to redeem the 1944 pledge of 'secondary education for all'. The people who campaigned for this before 1944 had something more in mind than that pupils should transfer to a different school building at 11 and have their school lives extended to 15 or even 16. Before 1944 the Board of Education Regulations for Secondary Schools said that a secondary school was for pupils who intended to remain there at least four years and up to at least the age of 16. It had to offer general education to an age range of at least 12 to 17 and had to offer instruction in English, at least one other language, geography, history, mathematics, science, drawing, singing, manual instruction or domestic subjects, and physical exercise. The most obvious mark of a secondary school, however, was that it offered courses leading to the School Leaving Certificate. Credits in certain subjects in this examination were recognized by universities and the professions as an entrance qualification. Secondary schools also prepared pupils between 16 and 18 for the Higher School Leaving Certificate. Before 1944 admission for the 1,400 schools of this kind was by examination, and competition was very keen. The schools had a recognizably secondary curriculum and were a recognized route to higher education and qualifications.

The 1944 Act extended 'secondary' education to the children who had hitherto remained in elementary schools, but was much more vague about what secondary meant. The local authorities had to provide sufficient schools offering secondary education, defined as 'full-time education suitable to the requirements of senior pupils'. A senior pupil was defined later as 'a person who has attained the age of 12 years but has not attained the age of 19 years'. This is not exactly a rigorous definition, and local authorities have a good deal of discretion. The fact that they have to provide for pupils up to 19, if parents and pupils want it, has allowed the very strong post-war movement called the 'trend': more children staying on after the statutory leaving age. But, as even conservative commentators agree, secondary education in the sense in which it was understood before 1944 is even now not available to all children over 11.

What happened was this. When the new notices went up outside schools proclaiming that they had been changed overnight from elementary to 'secondary modern' the Ministry of Education expected that they would offer 'a good all-round secondary education, not focused primarily on the traditional subjects of the school curriculum but developing out of the interests of the children.'* If the Ministry knew what it meant by this in the 1940s the Department is unlikely to claim to do so now. What was clear was that there was no determination that the secondary modern schools would be secondary in the pre-1944 sense. There were to be 'different types of secondary education'.

But if you have different types of secondary schools you have to have some method of deciding which children should go to

* *The New Secondary Education*, Ministry of Education Pamphlet No. 9, H.M.S.O., 1947. Reprinted 1958.

which. The heirs of the pre-1944 secondary schools, the grammar schools, remained the most attractive, and entry to them remained competitive. The process, universally known as the 11+ is described on page 116. A local authority had to note the number of grammar school places available and devise a scheme to fill these places and exclude everybody else. The process varied from one authority to another both in method and the proportion of children excluded.

The arrangement was defended on educational grounds. The distinguishing feature of grammar school courses, both before O level and in the sixth form, was held to lie 'in their length, in the scholarly treatment of their content and in the stern intellectual discipline' they afforded. Grammar schools were thus appropriate only for the intellectually able boy and girl. Indeed schools could do justice to the intellectually able only by segregating them early from their contemporaries and giving them special educational treatment. Left in the ordinary schools they would be held back, and they and the nation would suffer. Grammar school children were not to be otherwise privileged: there was to be 'parity of esteem' – and provision – in all kinds of secondary schools. The major assumptions behind all this were that levels of ability and intelligence remained roughly constant, at least after the age of 10 or 11, and that they could be measured accurately at that age.

The system caused dissatisfaction from the start, not surprisingly since three-quarters of the children were 'rejected' at 11+. Morale in all but exceptional secondary modern schools was low: an American visitor called them custodial rather than educational institutions. The growing number of secondary modern schools which achieved impressive G.C.E. results simply called the whole selection process into question. Parents objected, rightly, against the injustice of deciding a child's future at 11, particularly when the proportions of an age-group going to grammar schools varied widely from one local authority to another. The 11+ procedure was attacked by both psychologists and sociologists. Psychologists showed that intelligence and ability were not fixed, but depended upon a child's educational and social experience. An intelligence test score of 95 was not an exact measure, but an indication of a range of between 80 and 110: so selection based on test scores was crude to the point of injustice. And tests of intelligence measured verbal and arithmetical skills, rather than creativity, industriousness or good judgement, qualities which were at least equally important. Sociologists showed that the notion of a recognizable minority who alone were suitable for an academic, grammar school, education was equally unhelpful. The Crowther and Robbins reports both contained survey evidence of the reserves of talent in the population. Sociologists also showed how the 11+ procedure, while ostensibly educational, was effectively social; working class children were at a disadvantage.

The argument that the brighter children would be held back if taught with the others gave way before the evidence from scattered comprehensive schools in this country and from abroad. The most influential of the latter was the Stockholm experiment, in which half the city retained selection while the other half abolished it. The only group in the second half who did less well than their opposite numbers in the first were a small group of bright working class boys – and after two years even this difference was eliminated. What was striking was that in the non-selective half of the city all children of average and below average intelligence did very much better.

By the 1950s, the Labour Party, in pursuit of equality of opportunity, committed itself to the abolition of selection at 11+, and to a comprehensive system of secondary education. By this it meant that children should go to secondary schools as they do to primary schools, without previous selection, and that all secondary schools should offer a full range of secondary courses. When the party became the Government after the 1964 election, secondary reorganization was begun.

It is fair to say that few people in the Labour Party had any notion how selection was to be abolished. Most of the election propaganda was cautious, committing the party only to 'make a start'. The method chosen by the Department of Education and Science has been more effective than most people expected at the time. Circular 10/65 told local authorities that the Secretary of State 'requests' them 'to prepare and submit to him plans for reorganizing secondary education on comprehensive lines.' Successive Secretaries of State and their junior Ministers said that they had no power to compel local authorities to reorganize, and although they also equally insisted that legislation was not ruled out, the attempt was being made to reorganize by consent. A number of authorities had comprehensive schools already. Many counties had found that in rural areas separate grammar schools were too small to be sensible. Anglesey had gone completely comprehensive, Westmorland had tried (and had been prevented by a Labour Minister after the war!) and Devon was doing so gradually. Large urban authorities were building comprehensive schools where there were new housing estates: London, Coventry, and Bristol all had a large number of comprehensive schools by 1964.

Circular 10/65 gave a good deal of 'central guidance' on the methods by which reorganization could be achieved. It listed six forms of organization which 'have so far emerged from experience and discussion'. These were:

1) the 'orthodox' comprehensive school with an age-range of 11 to 18 – the 'all-through' school

2) a two-tier system where all pupils transfer at 11 to a junior comprehensive school and all go on at 13 or 14 to a senior comprehensive school

3) a two-tier system in which all pupils transfer to a junior comprehensive at 11, some transfer to a senior comprehensive at 13 or 14 and the rest remain in the junior (a version of this method had been used in Leicestershire: hence the 'Leicestershire plan')

4) a two-tier system in which all pupils transfer to a junior comprehensive at 11 and at 13 or 14 have the choice of a senior school which takes them well beyond the school leaving age and one which will not

5) comprehensive schools with an age-range of 11 to 16 combined with sixth form colleges for pupils over 16. (The Croydon authority toyed with this idea some years ago, hence the 'Croydon plan')

6) a three-tier system for the whole of school education, with

transfer from primary to comprehensive middle schools at 8 or 9 and from these to comprehensive senior schools at 12 or 13.

The circular said that methods 3 and 4 were not fully comprehensive, in that they retained separation of children at 13 or 14, and must be regarded as interim stages only. The other four methods were held to produce fully comprehensive schemes. On the whole this reorganization is being carried through without any specific building allocations. But under Labour no projects in the normal programmes were approved which would make reorganization more difficult, and authorities have adapted to reorganization the special building allocations for raising the school leaving age.

Reorganization is being opposed from two main points of view. There are those who still believe in selection and segregation at 11 plus, and others who wish to 'preserve' particular grammar schools. A group of the latter at Enfield were a notable irritant in the summer of 1967. The other opponents fasten on what they call 'hotch-potch' or 'botched up' schemes, where comprehensive schools are being established in buildings designed for something else. The Conservative Party said for many years that it would not withdraw Circular 10/65, but in fact did so, by Circular 10/70 within weeks of gaining office in 1970. More important was the new Government's decision to give priority to primary rather than secondary school building. This may have affected the pace, if not the direction, of reorganization. By the middle of 1971, 119 of the 163 local education authorities had schemes which provided for comprehensive schools in the whole or a greater part of their areas, and 16 had schemes covering a lesser part. About a dozen authorities were fully reorganized. Eight authorities have never submitted a scheme of reorganization and nine whose proposals were rejected have not put in revised plans. Since Circular 10/70 only two local authorities have withdrawn plans which had been previously approved in principle. No local authorities have proposed building new selective schools since the circular.

The pattern of reorganization is extremely varied. On the last figures available, 93 authorities with plans implemented or approved had schemes with all through schools, 50 with middle schools, 44 with two-tier arrangements and 31 with sixth form colleges. Some authorities, of course, have more than one kind of scheme in their areas.

Broadly the end of selection is now as 'national' a policy as can be expected. Coupled with the higher school leaving age in 1972 it gives promise that during the next decade the 1944 objective of secondary education for all will be realized – thirty years after. But we must now turn to secondary schools as they exist today.

Secondary Modern Schools

Most children in England and Wales go to secondary modern schools. These are the senior elementary schools of before 1944 – promoted. In 1969 there were 2,954 secondary modern schools taking over a million children and employing over 63,000 teachers, about 10 per cent of whom were graduates. They come in all sizes – there are 17 schools in the country with less than a hundred pupils and 24 with over a thousand – but schools of 200–300, 300–400, and 400–600, are extremely common. The average size of classes in secondary modern schools is 24·1, and the pupil-teacher ratio 18·9, but 40 per cent of the secondary modern classes in the country have more than 30 pupils. A child in a secondary modern school is more likely to be taught in a mixed class than in a single-sex class. Of the 2,954 schools, 487 are for boys only and 504 for girls only. There are places where the boys' and girls' classes are in different buildings round the same playground or where the boys and girls are in different ends of the same building. Sometimes, in a mixed school, the boys and girls will be taught separately for all or part of the time. For some subjects like physical education, domestic science, or metalwork they are bound to be taught separately.

When the secondary modern schools began in 1944 it was hoped that their teachers would experiment and discover what kind of education ought to be offered to the pupils in their charge. It is scarcely surprising in view of the vagueness of the early aspirations that the secondary modern schools as a whole have not achieved any distinctive ethos. Basically secondary modern schools have gone on offering the old elementary school curriculum, including religious knowledge, reading, writing and arithmetic, some elementary history and geography, and a certain amount of drawing, singing and physical education. This kind of education is secondary only in name. Many of the schools offer more. Some, while sticking to a very limited curriculum, nevertheless offer some opportunity for more advanced work perhaps up to the standard of an external examination. Some have pioneered the new Certificate of Secondary Education. Others have tended to specialize in one or more subjects outside the basic curriculum and have evolved special courses, probably with a vocational bias. A pupil might take arts and crafts, cooking, needlework, furnishing, rural science, music, seamanship, shorthand and typing, general science, or academic subjects for G.C.E. In a few secondary modern schools one can come across a fairly powerful science side or a devotion to foreign languages. In the academic year 1968–9 15 per cent of leavers from secondary modern schools attempted G.C.E. O level. One third of these got three or more passes, and only one in seven got five passes or more. Probably about 40 per cent of the secondary modern schools normally enter candidates.

Grammar Schools

The second largest number of children of secondary age go to grammar schools. Some people trace the ancestry of the grammar schools back to the time of Alfred the Great. Be this as it may, they are the heirs of the pre-1944 secondary schools. In 1969 there were 1,098 grammar schools taking 631,948 pupils taught by 35,000 teachers, about 75 per cent of them graduates. Like secondary modern schools they vary greatly in size but are, if anything, usually rather larger. Over three-quarters of them, for example, have between 400 and 800 pupils. The average size of classes in grammar schools is 20·9, and the pupil-teacher ratio 16·5. Just over a third of them are over the erstwhile maximum of 30. A child in a grammar school is very much more likely to be taught in a single-sex class than a mixed one. There are 361 boys' schools, 373 girls' schools, and 364 mixed.

THE SCHOOLS

The grammar schools are in many ways recognizably the secondary schools of before 1944, though their academic standards are higher. Children normally stay in them until the end of their fifth year (whereas many children leave secondary modern schools before the end of the fourth year) and are prepared for the G.C.E., which has succeeded the School Leaving Certificate, at O and A levels. The subjects normally offered include religious instruction, English language, English literature, modern languages (French usually, German often, Italian and Spanish rarely, and Russian almost never), Latin (very occasionally Greek), mathematics (pure and applied), chemistry, physics, biology, history, geography, art, music, woodwork, and metalwork for boys, housecraft for girls, and physical education. Some take additional subjects like engineering, architecture, economics, commercial subjects, and philosophy, and a few do things like gardening, agriculture and horticulture.

In addition to all this, most grammar schools have a flourishing group of 'out-of-school activities'. These may include a debating society, a music society, an art club, a museum, a history society, a geographical society, a chess club and a mountaineering society. Most of these will be organized by the pupils. Sport, which has a place in the time-table, spills over into after-school hours too. School teams play football or hockey matches on Saturdays and athletics training goes on in the long summer evenings. The boys' schools may also have a cadet force of some sort.

Miscellaneous

There are still comparatively few secondary schools which are neither secondary modern nor grammar – about 1,400 out of over 5,400. The most numerous single group are the comprehensive schools, of which there are 962. After them come a group of 109 technical schools. In the Department of Education's statistics for 1969 there are 331 'other secondary' schools, mostly central schools and curious groupings called multilateral and bilateral schools. In the 22 all age schools there were about 464 pupils of secondary school age.

Comprehensive Schools

Most of the comprehensive schools which exist today were started before secondary reorganization. Some of them are simply country secondary schools, some are large purpose-built comprehensives on new housing estates, others are housed in older buildings often some distance apart. Some of them are not fully comprehensive in that they 'compete' with a neighbouring grammar school and thus lose their most able potential pupils. There were 962 of them in 1969, with about 772,000 children and 40,000 teachers, of whom 25 per cent were graduates. They tend to be large: more than a quarter have over 1,000 pupils and nearly half of them have more than 800. The average size of class is 23·1 and the pupil-teacher ratio is 17·7. Most (771) of the schools are mixed, 94 are for boys only and 97 for girls only. These figures conceal the very wide variety of arrangements discussed on pages 90–92. They quite certainly underestimate the present extent of the move towards reorganization.

Technical Schools

Technical schools are the heirs to the junior technical schools of before 1944 which took pupils at 13 and prepared them for work in an industry or group of industries. The 109 in existence in 1969 were 181 fewer than six years before. They took under 56,000 pupils and employed 3,000 teachers, about a third of whom were graduates. They vary even more greatly in size than other secondary schools, but most of them have between 400 and 800 pupils. The average size of classes in technical schools is 21·5, and the pupil-teacher ratio 16·5. A child is nearly twice as likely to be in a single sex class as in a mixed class. There are 49 boys' schools, 21 girls' schools, and 39 mixed.

The fact that the number of technical schools is now falling (in some places it is official policy to close or change them) is in direct contrast to the hopes that were held for them before 1944. The Spens Report recommended that their numbers should be increased, that they should take pupils at 11 and that they should offer an alternative form of secondary education to the grammar schools. The Ministry of Education spoke of the schools in 1947 as being for a minority of able children who would do best if their curriculum were strongly coloured by industrial or commercial interests. Such were the expectations that educationists began speaking of the three kinds of secondary school which were available for the three kinds of secondary pupil – grammar, technical and modern. The word tripartite came to be used to describe the secondary system. Even now some educationists still talk as if a strictly tripartite organization were being replaced by comprehensive reorganization. In fact the tripartite system has never existed in more than a very few places.

It is hard to account for the failure of the technical schools to catch on. It is true that a lot of people in education have always thought them unnecessary, but they also have had very strong defenders. The chief difficulty was that although entry to them was competitive they remained overshadowed by the greater prestige of the grammar schools. Both parents and teachers tended to think of the technical schools as a second best. Some education authorities confirmed this by making it clear that children of a lower I.Q. could be accepted for technical schools after they had been rejected by the grammar schools. The impression was further confirmed by the fact that entry to technical schools remained at 13 and the grammar school rejects went to them after two years in a secondary modern school. The subordination of many of the schools to a technical college whose buildings they shared was another disadvantage in a system where the autonomy of the head teacher is prized.

As one might expect, the technical school curriculum is basically similar to that of a grammar school, though it may not offer Latin and Greek, or more than one foreign language. It is doubtful whether technical schools do more maths or sciences than grammar schools but they are certainly biased still towards particular trades like engineering or building. The pupils might get rather less history, geography, English literature and music, though art may take a higher, if industrially biased, place. Out-of-school activities may play a smaller part than in a grammar school.

Though the technical schools offer courses leading to G.C.E.

they also prepare pupils for other external examinations like the Royal Society of Arts Technical and Commercial Certificate examinations. Their close links with the technical colleges mean that many of their pupils will go on to take Ordinary and Higher National Certificates, rather than G.C.E. A level and a degree. Half of the teachers in technical schools are graduates, two-thirds as many as in grammar schools, and three times as many as in secondary modern schools.

Bilateral and Multilateral Schools

These curious titles describe curious arrangements. Briefly, the bilateral school is in effect two departments on the same site. For example, a grammar department and a technical school may together be called a bilateral grammar-technical school. Similarly, grammar, technical, and secondary modern departments may be built together, share, at different times, of course, the playing fields and swimming bath, and be called multilateral schools. The theory is that proximity will mean that transfer of pupils is easier between departments. In practice this is doubtful. These schools are now being swallowed up into other categories as secondary reorganization proceeds.

'Other Secondary' Schools

Most of the 331 'other secondary' schools known to the Department of Education are central schools left over from before 1944. A central school was one run under the Elementary School Code of Regulations, but which often had a commercial or industrial bias, and to which entrance was by examination. The central schools which still exist represent a sort of half-way house between the secondary modern and grammar schools.

Special Educational Treatment

Clearly if the local authorities are to offer such a variety of schools as are desirable in view of the abilities and aptitudes of the pupils, they must accommodate those pupils who suffer from any disability of mind or body. They must offer appropriate special educational treatment – either in special schools or otherwise. Ten categories of pupils requiring special educational treatment have been defined by the Secretary of State in the Handicapped Pupils and Special Schools Regulations of 1959. These are: the blind, partially sighted, deaf, partially hearing, delicate, educationally subnormal (E.S.N.), epileptic, maladjusted, physically handicapped, and those suffering from speech defects.

Every local education authority must ascertain what children in its area require special educational treatment. Any of its officers may give notice in writing to the parent of any child over 2 that the child must be submitted for examination by a medical officer of the authority. If a parent refuses to comply without reasonable excuse he may be fined up to £5. Equally the parent of any child over 2 can himself ask the authority to arrange for a medical examination. If the authority decides, as a result of the medical examination and any reports from teachers or others, that the child needs special educational treatment it must tell the parent of its decision and offer the treatment – either at a special school or otherwise. Though the upper limit of compulsory school age is 15 – and will be until 1972–3 – the compulsory school age for registered pupils at a special school is 16, and the pupil may remain there after that age if the parent and the authority so desire. Once a child is at a special school he may not be withdrawn without the consent of the authority, although in a dispute the parent may appeal to the Secretary of State.

It used to be the duty of the local education authority to ascertain what children in its area had such disability of mind as to make them unsuitable for education at school, and such children then became the responsibility of the local health authority. Since 1 April 1971 the power to exclude such children from education ceased, and local health authorities no longer have power to provide training for them. L.E.A.'s now have the same responsibility for mentally handicapped children as they have for other children and in particular those requiring special educational treatment.

The table on page 99 shows the number of children in each of the different kinds of special school.

SPECIAL EDUCATIONAL TREATMENT

SPECIAL SCHOOLS (maintained and direct grant)
1969

Category of handicapped pupil catered for in the school	No. of schools	No. of pupils	No. of full-time teachers
Blind	17	997	155
Partially sighted	20	1,554	150
Blind and partially sighted	2	225	30
Deaf	18	1,798	262
Partially hearing	5	500	67
Deaf and partially hearing	25	2,586	354
Deaf and partially sighted	1	178	20
Physically handicapped	79	5,586	588
Delicate	61	5,110	372
Delicate and physically handicapped	65	5,656*	502
Delicate and maladjusted	4	382	36
Maladjusted	100	3,730	545
Educationally subnormal	464	51,784	4,003
Epileptic	6	594	64
Speech defect	3	97	17
Multiple handicaps	2	62	6
In hospital	91	3,973	459
Total	963	84,812	7,630

* Including 109 partially sighted, 5 deaf, 76 partially hearing, 55 educationally subnormal, 281 maladjusted, 183 epileptic and 89 speech defect pupils

There are still regulations governing the maximum size of classes in special schools – 10 for deaf or partially hearing pupils or pupils suffering from speech defects; 15 for blind, partially sighted, or maladjusted pupils; 20 for a class of educationally subnormal, epileptic, or physically handicapped pupils; 30 for delicate pupils. By these standards 349 out of 5,508 classes for handicapped pupils were oversized in 1969.

THE SCHOOLS

Great advances have been made in the treatment of handicapped pupils despite the fact that there is a great deal still to be done in bringing existing schools up to modern standards. There are probably now very nearly enough places in special schools for children with the various kinds of physical handicaps. Children on waiting lists are there normally for only a short time, until they can be suitably placed. Provision over the country as a whole is, however, uneven and it is perfectly possible that particular areas might be short of places for particular groups of children.

There are certainly not enough places for maladjusted children, and the provision for the educationally subnormal and for children unsuitable for education in school is a positive scandal. In the first place, classes in ordinary schools are far too large for individual treatment to be given in them to educationally subnormal children. There are very few teachers in ordinary schools who have been specially trained for this job. This means that the schools put forward for transfer to special (E.S.N.) schools children who should ideally remain with them. Such children are often more able than those for whom the special schools are designed. If they do not get into special (E.S.N.) schools, they are simply returned to the ordinary schools which have already shown that they cannot handle them. If they *are* accepted they keep out other children who should be there. Probably an eighth of the children in these schools are unsuitable in this way, but there are nowhere near enough schools anyway. The Department of Education and Science has estimated that places in them are needed for 1·2 per cent of the school population. Over the country as a whole there are places for barely half this proportion. Only one or two authorities come anywhere near offering the required number of places. Even with a growing special building programme at least 10,000 more places will still be required. To teach the 350,000 'slow learners' in secondary schools some 17,500 teachers are needed. At present those being trained barely replace those who leave.

Until April 1971 children ascertained as unsuitable for education at school were the responsibility of the health authority. Training has been offered in centres, known as occupation centres or day training centres. Ideally these should have something like a nursery school regime. There are probably enough full-time or part-time centres for about three-quarters of the children who need them, but relatively few of these were designed and built for the purpose, and most are in converted premises. Residential care is often essential for the severely mentally handicapped child. This is available only in the mental deficiency hospitals. Recent research into the needs of these children suggests that the hospitals are not suitable for them, though they take some 8,500 children at present. What is worse, most of them are overcrowded. Large wards of fifty are common. Buildings are frequently unsuitable and training facilities inadequate. Within these limits, conditions vary enormously. In some hospitals the children's needs are understood and every effort is made to meet them: in others, conditions are little removed from Bedlam.

DIRECT GRANT SCHOOLS

The 315 direct grant schools are poised somewhere between independence and the state. Excluding special schools, all but 19 of them are grammar schools. Four are technical schools, and 15 are nursery schools. The direct grant grammar school has an independent governing body but is partly financed by a *per capita* grant direct from the Department of Education and Science (hence the name). It is governed by the Direct Grant School Regulations, 1959. Under these the school is independent of the local education authority but it is required, in return for its direct grant, to make a certain number of places available for the use of the authority. The authority pays the fees of the children who are allocated to the places they take. Each school must offer each year free places equal in number to at least 25 per cent of the previous year's intake. These free places are for children who have spent up to two years at a state primary school and can be allotted by the governors themselves or put at the disposal of the local authority, who will probably choose pupils through the local 11+ procedure. The local authority may also take 'reserve places' for suitably qualified children whether they have attended a state primary school or not. Unless the governors specifically agree, the number of free and reserve places should not come to more than 50 per cent of the previous year's intake. The remaining places in the school are called 'residuary'. These are allocated by the governors and paid for by the parents. But it is not just a question of giving the places to children whose parents can pay. The governors must be satisfied that the children have the same minimum educational standard as those occupying the free and reserve places. On the other hand there is the possibility of remitting fees for pupils in residuary places according to a means test, and these fees are covered by the Department. Here is how the tuition fees for direct grant schools were paid in 1969.

PAYMENT OF TUITION FEES FOR PUPILS IN UPPER SCHOOLS, 1969

	Number	Percentage
Free or reserved-place pupils		
Fees paid by local education authorities	60,734	60
Fees paid by governing bodies	1,140	1
Residuary-place pupils		
School Governors or endowed funds	255	—
Fees paid in full by parents and others	27,914	28
Fees wholly remitted by governing bodies	1,065	1
Fees partly remitted by governing bodies	10,526	10
Total	101,634	100

Altogether there are 176 direct grant grammar schools in England and Wales: 94 for girls; 80 for boys; and 2 mixed (the girls' schools include the 22 schools of the Girls' Public Day School Trust and 60 of the boys' schools belong to the Headmasters' Conference). Between them they take in their upper schools some 57,000 boys and 60,000 girls (or 117,000 altogether). There are 6,678 teachers, 65 per cent of whom are graduates. The schools tend to have between 400 and 800 pupils. The average size of class is 26·6, and the pupil-teacher ratio is 16·7. (In state grammar schools the ratio is 16·5 and in recognized independent schools it is 11·0).

Many direct grant schools have their own junior departments, but most of these are separate independent schools and the allocation of places is not governed by the Department's regulations. Well under a quarter of the children entering the upper schools in the autumn of 1967 had attended the junior departments, while five-eighths had been to state primary schools.

About 60 of the schools have boarding departments, but in 1969 these accounted for only 7,000 boys and 2,000 girls in the upper schools or under one-tenth of the total. There is no remission of fees for boarders as there may be for day pupils in residuary places but the tuition fees – of, say, £150 a year – are considerably (probably £100) lower than in independent boarding schools. This makes them very attractive to people who want a 'public school' education but do not want to pay for it.

Direct grant schools can take the most gifted children and they consequently have a generally high academic reputation. Direct grant schools frequently top the list of schools whose pupils get awards at Oxford and Cambridge. The second report of the Public Schools Commission showed that pupils at direct grant schools do proportionately better than those at state or other independent schools at G.C.E. A level and for entry to universities.

INDEPENDENT SCHOOLS

Registration

Since 1957 all independent schools have been brought under the eyes of the Department of Education and Science. On 30 September that year the Government introduced Part III of the Education Act, 1944. Proprietors of independent schools have had to apply for registration and the Department can refuse to register a school if the proprietor, staff, buildings, accommodation, or instruction given were not suitable. If anyone runs a school which is not registered he can be fined £20 for the first conviction or £50, three months' imprisonment, or both for a second or subsequent conviction. The independent schools have to tell the Secretary of State about the number of pupils by sex and age-groups; the number of boarders, if any, by sex groups; and the names, ages, and qualifications of the head and staff. If the proprietor of the school changes or the school moves, the Department must be told at once. Before they are registered all schools are inspected by Her Majesty's Inspectors. After a school has been registered it is still liable to inspection. If it does not come up to standard the Secretary of State can serve a notice of complaint specifying what he thinks is wrong and what he thinks should be done to put it right. If the school does not comply within a given time it can be struck off the register. The school can appeal to an independent schools' tribunal. Independent schools are not judged against the requirements laid down for state schools. Their staff and accommodation are considered on their merits. Since 1957 191 schools have had a notice of complaint served on them. Of these about half have subsequently satisfied the Department and the rest have either been closed or are still being considered. In January 1971 the Secretary of State announced she would ensure 'a steady rise in the standard required of all independent schools as a condition of registration'.

Recognition as Efficient

The only schools which were exempt from registration were those independent schools which were already recognized as efficient by the Ministry at the beginning of the autumn term 1957. Any independent school can apply to be recognized as efficient. Very roughly, a recognized school must be at least as well off for staff, accommodation, equipment, and so on as a comparable state school. For example, if the school claims to enter pupils for G.C.E. A level its staff must be properly qualified to teach to that level. The standards laid down for accommodation in state schools must be complied with. On the other hand, the Department is pretty broadminded and will tend to recognize a school as efficient if it is efficient according to its own announced standards. For example, a school may not believe in examinations. Provided it says so the Department will not insist on success at O level.

At the end of 1968 there were 1,448 independent schools recognized as efficient compared with the 1,476 independent schools which were not recognized. Most independent schools which might qualify for recognition do apply for it. The exceptions are those few schools which either feel themselves above it or which are so experimental that they feel the Department's standards are irrelevant. Recognized schools are normally proud of their status and display it prominently in their advertisements.

Nursery Schools

There is no need to add very much to the account of nursery schools on pages 80–83. There are only 11 independent nursery schools recognized as efficient, with 190 pupils and 22 full-time teachers. Oddly enough 7 of the children are boarders. These schools are virtually the same as state nursery schools. There are 107 unrecognized nursery schools with 2,120 full-time and 2,036 part time pupils and 215 full-time and 174 part-time teachers.

Independent Primary Schools

None of the types of independent schools quite corresponds to the state primary schools. This is chiefly because the age of transfer to an independent secondary school is as often as not 13 rather than 11. In its statistics the Department of Education and Science lumps all independent schools which are not secondary schools together and calls them all 'primary', regardless of the fact that some of them take children up to the age of 14. The nearest thing to a state primary school among independent schools is the pre-preparatory school, which may take children up to the age of 8 or even 11. But in the next stage, preparatory schools, the curriculum of fee-paying children differs radically from that of children in state schools.

The independent 'primary' schools are extremely varied. Half of the 744 recognized ones have under 100 pupils, and 58 of them have under 50 pupils. This means that the day school with one or two classes is quite usual, retaining still the atmosphere of an old print. Even the bigger schools are likely to be accommodated in what used to be large private houses. Just about one-third of the recognized primary schools are mixed: well over half of them are for boys. Very nearly all the 965 unrecognized schools are mixed.

There are very few girls' preparatory schools as such, but many independent girls' secondary schools have preparatory departments. There is an even greater number of schools which take boys and girls together up to say 11, and girls only from then on. The average number of pupils per full-time teacher in recognized primary schools is 13 and in unrecognized schools 14·8. Fees vary enormously: from as little as £40 a year for a day school to £500 a year for a boarding school.

Pre-preparatory Schools

As a broad generalization it is probably true that the pre-prep schools concentrate more on formal teaching than do state schools at this stage. Their pupil-teacher ratios are much more favourable, and in choosing them parents often argue that children learn to read, write, and do sums earlier than at state schools. It is difficult to say decisively how much this is due to the schools and how much to the home background. The most obvious mark of distinction of the independent pre-prep school is its uniform. State primary school children may be encouraged into a distinctive cap but they can seldom be uniformly got up in the hat, blazer, skirt, or trousers, sensible shoes and satchel which is the outward mark of the pre-prep school child.

Preparatory Schools

It is in the preparatory schools that the curriculum for fee-paying children differs most radically from that of children in state schools. Even when the demands of the 11+ bear heavily on state primary schools the 8-year-olds will still moderate their concentration on reading, writing, and arithmetic with a great deal of drawing, acting, movement, music, nature study, elementary history, and geography. In the preparatory school, boys at any rate will be embarking on their preparation for Common Entrance as soon as they enter at 8. They, too, will have English, but their arithmetic will be part of a mathematics course which includes geometry and algebra. They will start Latin and French – and perhaps Greek. They will be aware that scripture, geography, history, and science are examination subjects, as they are not in state schools. The task of the boys' preparatory school is theoretically to prepare the boy for his public school. More practically it is to prepare him for the Common Entrance examination.

Girls' preparatory schools have a task somewhere between that of the boys' prep schools and the primary schools. Many of their girls will take a Common Entrance examination at 11 and at that age will not have to offer French or Latin. The 11-year-olds need only English, arithmetic, and general knowledge. Girls entering at 12 will add French and an optional paper in simple mathematics; 13-year-olds add Latin too.

In both boys' and girls' prep schools, however, there will be very much more formal teaching than in primary schools. There will also be more organized games. In fact a primary school child is likely to be up and about in many of his normal school lessons and will no doubt have physical education, say, four times a week. The prep school boy is likely to be much more sedentary in his normal lessons and his physical exercise will be in the form of organized team games like rugger and cricket. Another big difference of course is that very many boys' preparatory schools are boarding schools.

The headmaster of a boys' prep school is likely to be an individual proprietor who has bought or inherited the school. He will almost certainly have under 200 pupils – well over half have under 100 pupils. The pupil-teacher ratio in the schools is as a whole about 14·7, and in over a third of them it is lower than this. The headmaster himself is more than likely to be a graduate, and nearly half of his staff will have degrees too. Recently the prep schools have been attracting officers coming out of the army at middle age, giving them a short training course. The headmaster's wife, if he has one, will normally be in charge of the domestic arrangements, or there will be a matron. Headmasters of prep schools which are recognized as efficient are eligible for membership of the Incorporated Association of Preparatory Schools. This started in the last century to decide the size of a cricket ball and now has a genial annual conference at Oxford, where the heads hear lectures on anything from 'leadership' to the bulk buying of sheets and pillowcases.

Independent Secondary Schools

Public Schools

In the autumn of 1961 the Minister of Education said in Parliament that he did not know what a public school was. In a sense the definition ought to be easy. A public school is either one of the nine recognized as such by the Clarendon Commission in 1861, or one which is run, not by a private proprietor, but by a governing body created by some statute, trust deed, or other scheme. In other words, the word 'public' is used either historically or to distinguish independent schools that might be held to be run in the public interest from those that are run primarily for financial profit to their owners. It is another historical accident that the state system has grown up and made the association of the word 'public' with independent schools rather inappropriate. Even so, confusion is not ended either by following the Clarendon Commission or by deciding that public schools are independent schools with governing bodies or trustees. Many progressive schools, for example, are controlled in this way; yet they neither call themselves public schools, nor are they thought of as public schools by most people. There are several associations to which independent schools belong and which are thought by some people to offer 'public-school status' to their members. So far as boys' schools are concerned the definition was settled by Mr (now Lord) Butler when he was President of the Board of Education and set up the Fleming Committee to consider the relationship of public schools to the state system. He then defined public schools as 'schools which are in membership of the Governing Bodies Association or Headmasters' Conference'.

INDEPENDENT SECONDARY SCHOOLS

The terms of reference of the Public Schools Commission (see page 111) repeated this definition.

The Headmasters' Conference is the older and more famous of the two. It was started by the headmaster of Uppingham in 1869 because he thought that Uppingham and other endowed grammar schools were threatened by Parliament. What he had in mind was an annual conference to defend the schools' freedom. In the first year only twelve headmasters turned up but in the second year thirty-four attended, including those of the nine schools recognized by the Clarendon Commission as public schools because they took boys from all over the country: Eton, Winchester, Westminster, Charterhouse, Harrow, Rugby, Shrewsbury, St Paul's and Merchant Taylors. Since that time the title 'public school' has rubbed off on to any school whose headmaster is elected to the Headmasters' Conference. The Conference itself is a closed and self-perpetuating body. It limits itself to some 200 members and accepts boys' schools only. In electing the headmaster the committee takes into account the statute, trust deed, or other scheme under which the school is controlled, the measure of independence of the headmaster, the size of the school, the number of old boys at 'Oxford and Cambridge or other British universities', the size of the sixth form, and 'the quality and variety of the school's work'. Although in theory it is the headmaster who is elected to the Conference, it would be astonishing if a new headmaster of a school whose previous head was a member were not elected. Again by historical accident the Headmasters' Conference still includes the heads of schools which are not really independent at all – two aided and five controlled schools. There are also 70 direct grant (including Scottish) schools in membership. The headmasters of a few state grammar schools have recently been elected.

The Governing Bodies Association was founded in 1941 and accepts as members the governing bodies of all schools taking boys – including, that is, co-educational schools. The association specifically states that it will admit independent schools, direct grant schools and 'others as it may determine'. It includes about 130 independent schools, sixty-five direct grant schools and eight 'others'.

THE SCHOOLS

By analogy girls' public schools are generally accepted as being those independent schools whose headmistresses are members of the Association of Headmistresses or the Association of Governing Bodies of Girls' Public Schools. The Public Schools Commission uses the latter. The trouble is that the Association of Headmistresses admits the heads of state schools to membership too. Nearly half of its members are in state schools, some of them in secondary modern and technical schools. The Association of Governing Bodies of Girls' Public Schools is limited to independent, direct grant schools, and 'others', like the Governing Bodies Association. It has at present about 140 independent schools and over sixty direct grant schools.

In the sense in which public schools have been discussed here, the best way of deciding whether a school is or is not a public school is simply to see whether it appears in the *Public and Preparatory Schools' Year Book* or the *Girls' School Year Book*. But unfortunately this isn't the end of the matter either. Many people would not recognize the aided schools which are members of the Headmasters' Conference as public schools in any obvious sense. Others exclude direct grant schools. Still more will not accept day schools as 'real' public schools. Others make invidious distinctions between 'major' and 'minor' public schools. Frankly, this is all so much nonsense: the distinctions have nothing whatever to do with the schools, their pupils, or with education, and are normally based on snobbery, ignorance and prejudice.

The public schools differ from state schools chiefly in physical respects. Only 22 of the 289 recognized public secondary schools are co-educational and only one in four of the unrecognized ones. Their entry is normally at 13, not at 11. Their staffing ratios are much more favourable (11·0 to 1 rather than 16·5 in state grammar schools and 18·9 in state secondary modern schools), though it should be remembered that in boarding schools the staff have considerably heavier duties which reduce this advantage. Their buildings and playing fields are likely to be much more extensive and their laboratories bigger, more numerous and better equipped. A good proportion of their pupils are boarders. The public schools also differ in that broadly they have a conscious aim which is variously expressed as developing character, inculcating sound religious sense and so on. But what is actually taught in formal lessons resembles pretty closely what is taught in state grammar schools. They are subject to the same pressures from the G.C.E. and from university entrance. Such differences as there are (in the emphasis placed on different subjects, for example, or in the degree of specialization) are between individual schools rather than between the public school as a group and the rest. The day may be differently organized, but once in the classroom the public schoolboy gets much the same treatment (if a little less skilled in some cases) as his contemporary in the state grammar school.

Other Independent Schools

The independent secondary schools which are not normally described as public schools fall into two types: first, those schools which are run as businesses by individual proprietors and which, it is probably safe to say, do what they can to imitate the public schools; and second, those schools which really deserve to be called independent in that they are experimental or progressive or just different.

The progressive school movement is difficult to describe now. The schools differ very much among themselves. For example, one school still enjoys the full flavour of 8-year-olds who smoke and call the headmaster by his nickname, while another reads out its successes in the G.C.E. at a formal school speech day. The truth probably is that the 'progressive' movement of pre-war days has been entirely successful. Its influence on state schools has been profound and it would be difficult to argue that there is today much less music, drama and art in traditional public schools than in progressive schools. Their obvious mark of distinction, in many cases, is that they are mixed boarding schools.

The Public Schools Commission

Late in 1965 the Secretary of State set up a Public Schools Commission under the chairmanship of Sir John Newsom. Its terms of reference were 'to advise on the best way of integrating the public schools with the state system of education'. For this purpose, the public schools were defined as 'those independent schools now in membership of the Headmaster's Conference, Governing Bodies Association or Governing Bodies of Girls' Schools Association'.

The Commission reported in July 1968. Its general conclusion was that independent schools were 'a divisive influence in society. The pupils, the schools and the country would benefit if they admitted children from a wider social background.' It recommended a scheme of integration by which some boarding schools offered at least half their places to assisted pupils needing boarding education, the detailed changes, which might take seven years, to be worked out by a Boarding Schools Corporation. The only justification for public expenditure on boarding education it said, should be the need for boarding, on social or academic grounds. On a rigorous interpretation of need, it thought there might be 80,000 children in England and Wales requiring places, 45,000 of whom should be in independent schools. Of these 20,000 places were already taken up wholly or partly at public expense. Guidance on boarding and placing policy should be given by the Corporation to regional consortia of local authorities. Assisted pupils should get tuition free up to the average cost of education in day schools, and parental contribution should be made to boarding and other costs. The full cost of each place would be paid by the Corporation. Taking up 45,000 places (plus 2,000 in Scotland) would cost £18½m. a year. An interim scheme for 32,000 places would cost £12½m. a year. This would be offset by savings of £6½m. a year for pupils assisted by the authorities under present arrangements.

Other recommendations included the following: that the schools should accommodate a wider range of ability, certainly to C.S.E. level and where possible below; that they should work closely with maintained schools, particularly in comprehensive schemes, sharing facilities; that some might accept aided school status, with a central body rather than a local authority; that there should be more co-educational boarding schools; that there should be an exchange of 100 teachers a year between maintained and independent boys' schools; in integrating schools there should be radical changes, towards mixed staff, alternative games, more spare time privacy for pupils, home contacts, freedom in dress and no beating and fagging; tax and other reliefs to charities which are not really charitable should be withdrawn and so should ways of paying fees other than from parents' income.

After presenting this report the Commission was reconstituted under its former vice-chairman, Professor David Donnison, to consider independent day schools and direct grant schools. It reported in January 1970 recommending that 'day schools receiving grants ... should participate in the movement towards comprehensive reorganization in ways that accord with local needs and plans' and that independent schools 'should be encouraged to participate in a comprehensive system' on similar terms. The report went into considerable detail about how this should be done.

The Labour Government took no action on either of these reports – except that the Chancellor of the Exchequer (in the Finance Act, 1968) had amalgamated the income of minors for tax purposes with that of their parents. In 1971 the Conservative Government reversed this provision – and the two reports of the Public Schools Commission must now be regarded as quite dead.

III) SUMMARY

If your child goes through the state system, he will start (legally) at 5, compete for a place in a grammar school at 11 (though *his* children will not!) and emerge at some time after 15. He will go to school, normally, with children from your neighbourhood, though if he goes to a grammar school he may have to travel a bit daily and will almost certainly be with a higher proportion of middle-class children than otherwise. His classes will be large: over forty perhaps at the beginning, and over thirty later on. When he is young, his teachers will normally be well trained and competent; when he is older they may be neither, though in a grammar school they will normally be pretty well educated. In the infant school the atmosphere will be free and encouraging; in the junior school streaming will set in and the 11+ will make its influence felt. His secondary modern school may be anything from a dreary or lawless failure to a bright, imaginative, or academically rigorous triumph. (A grammar school would probably get his head down quite soon to the G.C.E. and would assume that he was just as likely to stay on to 18 as not.) The curriculum will be rather basic most of the time, though there will be a conscious effort to bring in physical education and the arts. He may never get the chance to do foreign languages, any more than elementary science, or mathematics other than arithmetic – unless he goes to grammar school. He will almost certainly go to a day school and thus will escape the most vigorous attempts to give his school life 'tone' or 'tradition' or a particular religious slant. He is likely to meet girls often enough to discover that they are human. (If your child is a girl you need only make the relevant adjustments to this paragraph.)

If your child goes through the independent system, he may well start quite young, at 3 perhaps. He may have to compete to get into a preparatory school at 8 and into a public school at 13. He is very unlikely to leave much before 17. He will go to school, probably, away from home, perhaps from the age of 8, but will be educated almost exclusively among children from the same social class as yourself. His classes will be consistently small. When he is young his teachers may be badly trained and not very well educated, when he is older they will probably be neither. His school life is likely to be pretty formal throughout. He will have the Common Entrance Examination in mind from the day he enters preparatory school, and the G.C.E. and university entrance throughout public school. If he is in a boarding school he may be physically pretty uncomfortable. He will undergo compulsory team games. He will start foreign languages and mathematics at 8 or so, but will get only the most elementary science before 13. After that he might get a lot of it or something rather shoddy. He will be made very aware of 'the school', its 'tone', and 'tradition', and he may be told so frequently that he is a Christian as to get himself confirmed. He may find girls embarrassing. (If your child is a girl, this paragraph needs major adjustments: girls' schools vary more than boys' – and your daughter may go to one which tries to be a boys' public school or one which closely resembles a reasonable state day school.)

CHAPTER FIVE

Examinations
11+

PROBABLY the most famous aspect of English education is the 11+ examination. Most children still go through it – and so, in varying degrees of confidence, hope and dread, do their parents. It is one of the things that has flabbergasted, amused or horrified visitors from abroad. But until secondary reorganization is complete the purpose of the 11+ remains: to fit children of an area into the various secondary schools that are available there. Each local education authority devises its own scheme of selection: there is no national examination and, despite what many people still seem to think, there was no mention of 11+ in the 1944 Act. It may be added that probably many children of the relevant age (about 10½) enjoy doing the tests set. But as one headmistress has added, 'If only their future did not depend on it'.

What of the examination itself? What does it consist of? As each local education authority runs its own, a general answer is difficult, though not impossible. Similar methods are used by most authorities: they differ in the importance they attach to particular methods and in the combination of methods they use. Methods include tests, teachers' assessments, a 'quota' system, and interviews (of children and sometimes their parents). The tests may include verbal reasoning or intelligence tests, tests in English and arithmetic, English essays, non-verbal tests, mixed verbal and non-verbal tests, special and other tests. The tests, of almost every sort, may be standardized or unstandardized. Of all the methods, the tests are the one that bewilder parents the most, though their 'results' are the least complicated and ambiguous of the lot. If you must select children, the standardized tests are the fairest and most dependable way of doing it.

The Tests

Many of the standardized tests used by local authorities are compiled by the National Foundation for Educational Research,

THE TESTS

or the Godfrey Thomson Unit for Educational Research at the University of Edinburgh (the 'Moray House' tests). Actual examples of them may not be given, but the following give an idea of the tests used in English, arithmetic, and verbal reasoning. The children are given half or three-quarters of an hour for each paper, which may contain 50 or 100 short questions.

English:

(1–3) One word in each sentence below is left unfinished. Write this word in full in the bracket at the side, taking care to spell it carefully.

    1. A person who can't hear is d———   (........)

    2. Windsor C——— is the home of the Queen   (........)

    3. Mary took her raincoat in c——— it rained   (........)

(4–9) In each line below a sentence has been started for you. Write some more words to finish each sentence. The first one has been done for you.

    4. Although he disliked *running, he entered every race.*

    5. Because of ....

    6. Since hearing from ....

    7. Crying with ....

    8. To the astonishment of ....

    9. After waiting for more than ....

(10–15) Put the necessary punctuation marks in the sentence below. Mark the words which should begin with capital letters like this – <u>friday</u>

In each case the marks will be one of these , . " " ?

    Where is john that naughty boy demanded the teacher

(16–17) Change these sentences to the past, by writing ONE word in each empty space.

    16. Today I sing in my bath because I feel happy.
        Yesterday I ...... in my bath because I ...... happy.

    17. Later on I shall go out and spend my pocket money.
        Earlier today I ...... out and ...... my pocket money.

EXAMINATIONS

(18–25) Read through this passage and answer the questions below.

> A year ago, a large red-faced farmer went to Shrewsbury market on his old grey mare. Behind him rode his comely daughter. As they approached a crossroads a large black raven who had concealed himself in the foliage of a tree suddenly cried 'Croak!' The aged mare was so terrified that she fell down and broke her leg, and the farmer was thrown to the ground and struck his head on a stone. The raven flew off, quite content with the trouble he had caused.

In Numbers 18 to 22 underline the one correct answer in brackets.

18. This story is about
    (Shrewsbury/a wicked raven/a journey/birds/mares).

19. The farmer was
    (rich/old/big/frightened/lost).

20. The raven was
    (invisible/mischievous/noisy/helpful/walking).

21. The raven hid
    (behind a bush/by the roadside/all the time/among the leaves of a tree/with a friend).

22. All this happened
    (today/yesterday/some years ago/twelve months ago/never).

23. Write one word from the passage which means 'beautiful'.

24. Write one word from the passage which means 'very frightened'.

25. Write one word from the passage which means 'satisfied'.

Arithmetic:

1. Add
   28
   15
   36
   —

2. Subtract
   £ s d
   15 0 5
    8 3 6
   ———

3. Multiply
   Yds ft ins
   74 3 5
          5
   ———

4. Divide
   Stones lbs ozs
   9) 29   9   2

5. Take 19 from 37 and divide the answer by 6.

THE TESTS

6. Write in figures two thousand and twelve.

7. If oranges are 3 for 10d., how many oranges shall I get for 3s. 4d.?

8. Our family uses 16 pints of milk a week. How many *gallons* do we use in a year?

9. In which of the following numbers does 7 represent the largest quantity? 675   487   1578   710

10. If there are 1760 yds to a mile, how many *feet* are there in a quarter of a mile?

Verbal Reasoning:

1. Underline the right answer in the brackets.
   In is to out as up is to (top/bottom/down/through/hole)

2. Underline the TWO words which mean something different from the rest.
   daisy/weed/chrysanthemum/flower/tulip/daffodil

3. Write ONE letter in the brackets to finish the first word and start the last.
   REN(..)EA

4. Fill in the missing number below.
   36, 27, (..), 9

5. If 29384791 means STRENGTH, what does 184 mean?

6. Underline the TWO words in the brackets which ALWAYS go with the word outside:
   TREE (park/leaves/birds/bushes/branches)

7. Underline the TWO words which must change places to make this sentence sensible:
   The cows milks the farmer

8. Write TWO letters in the brackets to continue the series:
   A Z Y A X W A V U (..) (..)

9. Write a word in the empty brackets so that the three things on the right go together like the three things on the left:
   girl (two) feet :: horse (......) hooves

10. Underline TWO words, one from each bracket, that mean most nearly the OPPOSITE of each other:
    (leave, run, start) (walk, finish, go)

Who Uses What

Which authorities use what methods and in what combinations is an absurdly guarded secret. The National Foundation for Educational Research knows but has promised not to tell. This is because local education authorities in general say that publishing their procedures in a way in which they could be compared would re-awaken anxieties and demands among parents which would otherwise die away. Some authorities say that their procedure is far too complicated to be stated briefly (one chief education officer has said that he would need at least 2,000 words to explain his) and others hint that the really important decisions cannot be explained in actual words. Some authorities make no effort whatever to explain to parents what is going to be done to their children, though they claim to be prepared to explain if anyone calls round at the education office. The best that can be done for the moment therefore is to say what the position is generally. The fullest account is in *Admission to Grammar Schools* by A. Yates and D. A. Pidgeon, and there are two pamphlets published by the National Foundation for Educational Research, called *Procedures for the Allocation of Pupils in Secondary Education* and *Local Authority Practices in the Allocation of Pupils to Secondary Schools*.

Very nearly all authorities use verbal intelligence, or verbal reasoning tests. The exceptions are mostly Welsh, and they have language difficulties. Equally, most authorities use tests of attainment in English and arithmetic, but some authorities seem to be abandoning them in favour of relying on the assessments of primary school teachers in these subjects. Almost no authorities use unstandardized tests alone, but there are still a number which use a combination of standardized and unstandardized tests. One hears that the use of English essays is declining again after a brief moment of popularity. There has never been any agreement about how essays can best be marked. One in ten authorities do not mark essays at all, and a third of them mark only some of the essays. Most authorities give the children a choice of topics for the essay and most also use a pool of examiners in marking. Primary school teachers' assessments are used for all children by about two-thirds of the authorities. The assessments may be expressed as orders of merit or as grades – or both. Most authorities ask the teachers for over-all assessments and over half of them ask for the teachers to take personal qualities into account. Some ask for separate assessments of attainment, and a quarter of them ask the teachers to take the home background into account and make allowances for age. The number of authorities who interview children has recently been declining. The interviews may be conducted by the primary school heads, secondary teachers, psychologists, administrators, inspectors, or members of the education committee, or by various combinations of these.

Over three-quarters of the authorities have a 'border zone' procedure for those children who are difficult to classify first time round. Some give extra tests or refer the child to a psychologist. Many consult primary school record cards and some use an interview.

Even with present plans for secondary reorganization the 11+ examination is far from being abolished.

Common Entrance

The Common Examination for Entrance to Public Schools, normally known as Common Entrance, is the qualifying examination for entry to most of the schools of the Headmasters' Conference and to many independent boys' schools outside it. During the last few years there has been a radical revision of the examination and a good deal of change in the curriculum of the preparatory schools. The first examinations with the new papers were in the autumn of 1968, and the most obvious change – the introduction of a science paper – occurred in 1969. Under the new scheme there are three groups of papers, groups A, B and C. The first contains compulsory papers, in English, mathematics (two in each) and French. Group B is of 'compulsory supporting' papers, which are used not to decide whether a boy has passed but to place him in the appropriate class or set in the new school. In this group there are papers in history, scripture (two alternatives each) and geography. Group C is of optional papers – in Latin, mathematics, Greek and science. Science will move into group B in 1971. These changes underline the importance of the examination not only for entrance to public schools but as a leaving examination for preparatory schools. Apart from the introduction of science, the most important changes are a new approach to mathematics, a more liberal approach to English, a more oral emphasis in French and a shorter outline period in history. The papers are 45 minutes or an hour long – and the preamble to the seventh edition of Curriculum for the Preparatory Schools lays down the 'fundamental requirements' of good speech, spelling, handwriting and presentation in school work and in the examination.

The papers are set and assessed by assistant masters at public schools. They are appointed by the Board of Managers of the examination, which is made up of a chairman and three representatives of the Headmasters' Conference and three of the Incorporated Association of Preparatory Schools. The Board finally assesses the papers. Neither the Board nor the examiners mark the answers. The marking is done by the school at which a candidate is registered. Scholarships are rarely awarded on the results of Common Entrance but candidates for them are examined quite separately. The papers are set and marked by the school offering the scholarships.

There are three sittings of Common Entrance every year – in February, June and November. In 1969–70, 1,821 sat in November, 1,238 in February and 5,821 in June. A boy who fails the examination may take it again if he hasn't reached the age limit of 14 and if permission is given by the headmaster of the school for which he is sitting. Boys are not normally encouraged to make a second attempt unless there are special reasons for the first failure.

A description of the examination, however, is by no means a discussion of the whole process of entry to public schools. For some of them competition is so intense that parents have to think far ahead. Leaving aside those schools at which a boy has to be registered before he is one year old, there are many other places where a choice has to be made before a boy's interests are formed or his capacities guessed at. Parents tend to put their sons' names down for two or three schools of varying outlook and academic standard. Clearly an early choice of preparatory school must be made, especially if parents want a day school.

The boy starts at his prep school when he is 8. When he is 10 or 11 his headmaster will feel able to assess his chances and guide his parents in a final choice of school. At the same time public schools draw up their definite lists and ask the preparatory schools to confirm that the boys are likely to be up to their standard in two years' time. Not all parents narrow their choice to one at this stage. Some keep two schools in mind. Sometimes the schools may cooperate and the boy's papers can be passed to the second if he fails at the first.

The schools do not publish their pass marks (but they will tell you if asked) and these vary from below 50 to above 60 per cent. Since each school does its own marking, one school's 50 per cent may not be at all the same as another's. If a school has offered a definite place, it may exert itself to make a boy's papers reach the required standard. Some schools turn away only one or two boys a year. Others have a failure rate of 10 per cent or more. After the June sitting the assistant secretary of the Incorporated Association of Preparatory Schools may get three dozen urgent pleas for help in placing rejected boys (there are over 5,000 candidates at that sitting). The I.A.P.S. has built up an unofficial clearing house of places and many of the rejected get in quite quickly elsewhere. Not all the boys who want to go to H.M.C. schools eventually do so, but pretty well all of them get into these or other independent schools.

Although the over-all failure rate in Common Entrance itself is clearly not high, the number of boys rejected by the public schools is higher than this suggests, because of the tacit selection process made earlier when the boys are only 11. But even when this is allowed for there is a great difference between the selection examinations for independent and for state schools. Only a quarter of an age group is admitted to state grammar schools. Between 80 and 90 per cent at the very least of those seeking admission are accepted by public schools. Even allowing for enormous differences of homes and backgrounds it is clear that the public schools take a wider range of ability than state grammar schools. The most reliable guess suggests that at least a fifth of the boys in public schools are of a lower I.Q. than would normally be needed to get into a state grammar school.

There have often been tentative proposals for making it possible for more and different children to go to public schools. The difference between the age at which pupils take Common Entrance and that at which they take the 11+ is one obvious handicap. Another is that Common Entrance contains subjects like scripture, Latin and especially the compulsory French, which a boy in a state school is unlikely to have spent enough time on – certainly in the primary school and perhaps even in two years at a grammar school – to feel at home with Common Entrance papers.

The Questions

Here are some examples of questions to be set in the new Common Entrance Papers. One question has been taken from each of the revised specimen papers recommended by a working party and published in July 1967. They are quoted with kind permission.

Group A – Compulsory Papers

English: A 600-word passage from William Golding's *Lord of the Flies* is followed by ten questions:
  1. What part of speech in its context is each of the 6 words underlined?
  2. Explain the meaning of FOUR of the following words as used in its context, indicating in each case which word you are explaining:
     humid, unheeding, gaudy, furtive, avidly, pallor.
  3. Why was Jack 'bent double'?
  4. With what weapons did Jack set out pig-hunting?
  5. In what way was the forest 'uncommunicative'?
  6. What is meant by 'The silence of the forest was more oppressive than the heat'?
  7. What three clues led Jack to the pig?
  8. Why are the masses of creeper said to be 'inscrutable'?
  9. Did Jack kill a pig on this occasion? What is the evidence?

THE QUESTIONS

10. Write down three phrases or sentences from the passage which help to suggest that the forest had a personality of its own.

English II: You are required to write on ONE of the following. You should aim at writing 2 sides of examination paper.

1. A rich uncle has unexpectedly left you £1000. Describe how you spent it.
2. What famous person would you most like to meet? Describe how you actually meet him, what you say to each other, and what you think of him in the flesh.
3. Describe a visit to one of the following: a cathedral, a castle, a lighthouse, a fair, a circus, a point-to-point.
4. A Day to Remember.
5. The Street.
6. Food and Drink.

Mathematics I: A ship steams 10 n.mi. on a bearing of 067°, and a further 8 n.mi. on a bearing 135°. By means of an accurate drawing find the distance of the ship from its starting point and the bearing on which it must sail to return by the most direct route.

Mathematics II (Tables or slide rules may be used in this question):
   (i) Find the square of 9·5
   (ii) Find the square root of 576
   (iii) Find the hypotenuse of a right-angled triangle in which the sides containing the right angle are 3·5 cm. and 4·2 cm. (Give the length to a reasonable degree of accuracy.)

French: (1) Ecrivez:
   Au négative: Il a un chapeau,
   Au futur: Je le crois quand je le vois, mais je sais que ce n'est pas vrai,
   Au pluriel: Le nouvel élève, celui qui n'a pas de crayon.

(2) Ecrivez le contraire de:
   Rapidement – commencer – bon – juste – l'hiver.

(3) Répondez à l'affirmatif en remplaçant les noms par des pronoms personnels:
   (i) Est-ce que *les filles* ont prêté *leurs poupées aux voisines*?
   (ii) Vous promenez-vous *en ville* avec *votre père*?

EXAMINATIONS

Group B – Compulsory Supporting Papers

History, 55 BC–1603 (see below for alternative): Answer *one* of the following questions:

1. Tell the life story of Alfred the Great.
2. Write an eye-witness account of the Battle of Agincourt as seen by a French knight.
3. What were the problems that faced Queen Elizabeth I during her reign and how successful was she in dealing with them?
4. Write an account of the dress and amusements of the various classes of English society in the fourteenth century.

History, 1485–1945 (alternative to above): Choose *four* of the following and say briefly what you know of them:

The Pilgrimage of Grace – The New Model Army – The South Sea Bubble – Quiberon Bay – The Anti-Corn-Law League – Battle of Britain.

Scripture (see below for alternative): *Either:* Write a brief life story of Moses or David. *Or:* Write down three occasions when God saved His people from their enemies, through the courage of men who put their trust in Him; and tell one of the stories as fully as you can.

New Testament and Religious Knowledge (alternative to above): What did Jesus teach about God's forgiveness of sinners, and about our forgiveness of other people? What does this mean in the world today?

Geography: This table gives average monthly climatic figures for Winnipeg (Canada):

temperature:

	J	F	M	A	M	J	J	A	S	O	N	D
°C.	−17	−16	−7	3	11	17	20	19	13	6	−5	−13
°F.	1	4	19	38	52	62	68	66	55	43	23	8

Precipitation inches:

0·9	0·8	1·1	1·2	2·1	2·6	2·7	2·5	2·3	1·4	1·1	0·9

1. Which is the hottest month? Which is the wettest month? What is the annual range of temperature?
2. Why is it better to use 'precipitation' rather than 'rainfall' in the table?
3. What name is given to this type of climate?
4. Explain as fully as you can how this climate influences (i) farming activities, (ii) transport, (iii) the construction of houses in the region?

THE QUESTIONS

Group C – Optional Papers

Latin: Translate this passage into English, and then answer the questions underneath:

Daedalus *artifex* erat per totam Graeciam notus. Templa aedificavit, deorum statuas miras pulchrasque fecit. Tum, quod sororis filium necaverat, a iudicibus condemnatus ad insulam Cretam abiit. Diu Daedalus cum filio Icaro captivus a rege tenebatur. Sed tandem *alas* facere constituit, ut effugere possent. Postquam multa milia passuum volaverunt, Icarus in mare cedidit. Daedalus tamen ad Italiam advenit, ubi deo Apollini alas dedicavit.

artifex = craftsman.   ala = wing.

1. Give one English word derived from the root of each of the following Latin words: iudicibus, tenebatur, constituit.
2. Express in Latin in the passive: *Templa aedificavit*.
3. Express in Latin in the active: *Daedalus a rege tenebatur*.
4. What case is *filio*? How do you know?
5. What part of what verb is *possent*?
6. Give the principal parts of the verb from which *cecidit* comes.

Mathematics III: Say which of the following statements are true; if you think a statement is wrong, suggest how it could be corrected:

1. $\sqrt{2} \simeq 1\cdot414$.
2. $(a + 3)(b - 2) = ab - 3a + 2b - 6$.
3. If $2^x = 64$, then $x = 5$.
4. The gradient of the line joining (2, 1) and (7, 4) is 5/3.
5. If $A \cup B = A$, then $B \subset A$.

Science: Some people can make a fire by rapidly twisting a dry stick while one end of the stick is pressed against soft wood, and is covered with dry leaves. The leaves get warmed up so much that they catch fire:

1. Describe the energy changes that are taking place when the leaves are being warmed.
2. Much more heat is produced when the leaves catch fire. Where does this heat come from?
3. An easier way of making a flame is to rub a match on a matchbox. You use much less energy than you do when you make a flame by rubbing a stick on wood. Why is the same result produced with much less energy?

4. You are given a box of matches and a piece of copper wire the same length and size as a match. Using no other apparatus, how would you show, to your own satisfaction, that copper conducts heat better than wood does? Say exactly what you would do and what you would notice.

Greek: The working party recommends that the Greek paper remain unchanged for the present. This example is from a past paper. Put into Greek:

1. The brother of the sailor is not brave.

2. We ordered all the prisoners to leave the ships which the allies wished to send.

3. He said that the men in the island would fight so well that we should not be able to capture it.

GENERAL CERTIFICATE OF EDUCATION

The general certificate of education – the G.C.E. – has been the most important external examination in secondary schools. An external examination is one which is set and marked by people outside the school or education office, and the teachers see the papers for the first time when they hand them out to their pupils. The universities took the initiative in founding and running the first examining boards over a hundred years ago, and they are still responsible for running six of the eight examining boards which now exist. These boards are: Associated Examining Board for the General Certificate of Education, University of Cambridge Local Examinations Syndicate, Northern Universities' Joint Matriculation Board (the Universities of Manchester, Liverpool, Leeds, Sheffield and Birmingham), University of London University Entrance and School Examinations Council, Oxford and Cambridge Schools Examination Board, Oxford Delegacy of Local Examinations, Southern Universities' Joint Board for School Examinations (Universities of Bristol, Exeter, Reading and Southampton), Welsh Joint Education Committee. (All but the first and last of these are university boards.)

Each board makes its own syllabuses, sets its own question papers and publishes lists of results. It is possible, therefore, that the types of papers set may vary from one board to another and, perhaps more important, that standards may differ. On the other hand the certificates issued by all the boards are recognized by universities and professional bodies and the boards constantly try to see that their examinations are comparable. For example, the chief examiners of all the boards see the syllabuses and actual scripts from a past examination of the other boards and meet to discuss them. Over-all supervision of the examination system is the responsibility of the Schools Council for the Curriculum and Examinations.

It was in 1951 that the G.C.E. replaced the previous School Certificate and Higher School Certificate examinations. This change was more than one of name. It introduced the most distinctive feature of the G.C.E. The old School Certificate demanded passes in specific groups of subjects. Without the right number and combination a pupil did not get a certificate. In the G.C.E. a pupil gets a certificate recording whatever successes he has, whether there are nine of these or only one.

The examination is held at two levels, the Ordinary (O) and Advanced (A). Pupils normally take O level at the end of their fifth year in a secondary school, that is at about the age of 16. They take A level after two years in a sixth form, that is about the age of 18. But candidates may enter for different subjects at different dates, and may enter for the same subject more than once. In some schools pupils take their O level in stages or even ignore O level altogether in those subjects that they are going on to take at A level. Passes in individual subjects at A level are graded A to E in descending order of merit – and these grades are used by universities in deciding whether to admit students. Candidates who fail a subject at A level may, if their marks are good enough, be awarded an O level pass in that subject. Candidates sitting A level in a subject may attempt 'special' papers in that subject (except in craft and practical subjects). Passes are not awarded in 'special' papers but candidates can earn a supplementary grading, like 'distinction' or 'merit'. Marks gained in them are taken into account by local authorities in awarding scholarships and by universities and other institutions of higher education in offering places.

EXAMINATIONS

Most boards hold examinations at O and A levels in the summer and a second O level in the autumn. Only London and the Associated Examining Board have a second A level and these are held in January. In the summer of 1969, forty-six different subjects or groups of subjects were taken at O level and thirty-eight at A level. Easily the most popular single subject was English language at O level, which was taken by 355,337 boys and girls. Something over a half of these passed. Some 225,179 boys and girls entered for O level maths and a slightly lower proportion passed than for English. The single subject which attracted the smallest number of entries was Welsh: 692 boys and girls sat, three-quarters of them boys, and 66 per cent of them passed. The most popular single subject at A level in 1969 was English literature. Over 53,000 boys and girls entered and three-quarters of them passed. The next most popular was physics with 40,630 entries, over two-thirds of whom passed. History came next with 35,000 entries, nearly three-quarters of whom passed. Maths are rather muddling. At A level there are papers in pure maths, applied maths, pure and applied maths, 'maths counting as a double subject' and 'further maths'. The total number taking maths of all kinds at A level came to something like 61,000.

The Papers

Here are some examples of questions set in the General Certificate of Education at O and A levels. They are all taken from a summer examination of one board, the Associated Examining Board, and are quoted with the Board's kind permission.

O Level

English Language I: Choose *one* of the following subjects for composition. About *one hour* should be spent on this question:

1. The importance of the wheel.
2. Describe the attractions of your favourite month of the year *or* your favourite county *or* your favourite Sunday newspaper.
3. You have investigated the leisure activities of the boys or girls in your age-group. Write out your report.
4. Science in the service of agriculture *or* building *or* aviation.
5. Show that the running of a home efficiently is a skilled occupation.

THE PAPERS

6. An historical novel *or* a detective story *or* an adventure story that you enjoyed reading and the reasons why it appealed to you.

7. Tell the story of the relief of a village that had been isolated owing to severe floods or to a heavy fall of snow.

English Language II: Write a summary of the following passage in not more than 110 words, taking care to give a continuous connection of ideas, and using your own words as far as possible. State at the end of your summary the number of words you have used. The passage contains about 320 words.

(The passage set was from *English Social History*, by G. M. Trevelyan.)

English Literature: (These are questions on prescribed books. Candidates are to answer not more than *two* questions in the first example and *one* of the questions in the second.)

Macbeth:

1. How do Macbeth's actions influence the conduct of Macduff? What part is played by the latter in the invasion of Scotland and the overthrow of Macbeth?

2. Give a brief account of two episodes when the play seems to move comparatively slowly, and explain what purposes they serve.

3. What do you learn of the character of Macbeth from his behaviour (i) before he meets his wife at his castle, and (ii) on the night of the murder before the apparition of the dagger?

The History of Mr Polly:

Either (i) Describe the window-dressing episode, taking care to bring out the humour.

Or (ii) Explain why Mr Polly was such a success with the Larkins family before his marriage, and yet failed to rouse any affection in Miriam after his marriage.

Geography: With the help of a sketch-map, describe the position and site of London. Use this to explain the development of London.

(i) as a port;

(ii) as a capital city;

(iii) as one of the greatest industrial cities of the world.

EXAMINATIONS

History: (There is a choice of periods in English, European, or some other regional history.)

   6. What problems had Henry IV to solve on his accession and how successful was he in solving them?

   39. Describe the main features of the history of the Labour Party between the two world wars.

Mathematics: Arithmetic: (i) The average age of a class of twenty-two boys is 14 years 4 months. If the class is joined by two boys whose ages are 15 years 1 month and 15 years 7 months, find the new average age of the class.

(ii) A rectangular picture, 16 in. by 12 in., is surrounded by a wooden frame $\frac{1}{2}$ in. wide. Find the area of the frame.

Mathematics: Algebra: (i) A firm employs x men and y boys. The men are paid £p each per week and the boys £q each per week. Find the average payment per person per week.

(ii) If v varies inversely as t and $v = 12$ when $t = 6$, find the value of t when $v = 18$.

Mathematics: Geometry: (i) A rhombus $ABCD$ and an equilateral triangle ABE are drawn on opposite sides of AB. If the angle $BAD = 144°$, calculate the sizes of the angles DAE, AED, and EBD.

(ii) In a pentagon $PQRST$, angle TPQ = angle $PQR = 90°$, angle $RST = 152°$ and angle STP = angle SRQ. Calculate the size of the angle SRQ.

French: Translate into French:

The old farmer opened the letter with trembling fingers. This is what he read: 'I have nearly finished my military service. I shall leave my regiment soon and I shall arrive in Marseilles at the beginning of September. I shall be very pleased to see you again.

ANDRÉ.'

Toussaint, the farmer, said to himself, 'He is going to come home at last. He left us nearly two years ago. We shall be very pleased to see our son again.'

On the 7th September, the farmer was up very early. He dressed quickly and set off for the station. He arrived there a little before 8 a.m. Toussaint had an impatient nature and he kept looking at his watch. At last the sound of a train could be heard. 'I wonder if he has changed very much,' said the old countryman to himself. The train came into the station. Toussaint heard a familiar voice. He looked at the compartment in front of him and there stood André, whom he had not seen for such a long time.

Physics: According to the simple kinetic theory all matter consists of molecules. In terms of this theory, write short notes on

1. the fundamental differences between liquids and solids,
2. latent heat of evaporation of a liquid,
3. expansion,
4. the increase of pressure when a gas is heated at constant volume,
5. the Absolute Zero of temperature,
6. the difference between heat and temperature.

Chemistry: Describe the manufacture and purification of coal gas. Name the principal by-products of this process and give one important use of each.

Human Biology: Draw a labelled diagram of the female human reproductive system and indicate on it the usual position in which (i) semen is deposited, (ii) fertilization takes place, (iii) an ovum is formed, and (iv) the embryo is housed.
What determines the sex of an embryo?

A Level

English Essay: You are advised to spend about one and a half hours on the question and to revise your essay carefully. Choose one of the following subjects:

1. Tricks of the trade.
2. The English Channel: a tunnel, a bridge, or neither?
3. The agriculture of the country in which you live – its prospects and problems.
4. Tradition and experiment in architecture or in any other fine art.
5. Rebels.
6. 'A country's reading public gets the Press it deserves.' Give two opposing points of view in a debate on this motion.
7. Patent medicines.
8. 'One crowded hour of glorious life.'

Geography: Discuss the geographical aspects of one of the following topics:

1. Benelux,
2. Norden,
3. The European Coal and Steel Community,
4. The Neutrality of Switzerland.

History: (again there are different periods which can be chosen.) Why was British public opinion sympathetic to the policies of Franklin D. Roosevelt between 1933 and 1939?

Mathematics: (i) Differentiate $\dfrac{xe^{x2}}{(1-x)ex}$ with respect to x.

(ii) If $y = a \cos(\log x) + b \sin(\log x)$, show that
$$x^2 \frac{d^2y}{dx^2} \times x \frac{dy}{dx} + y = 0.$$

Physics: Describe with a diagram and with the relevant theory a terrestrial method for determining the velocity of light.

Give reasons why it is important in science to know accurately the velocity of light.

University Entrance

The importance of the G.C.E. lies in the fact that success in it at some level is recognized as a minimum qualification for entry to universities, colleges and professional bodies. To get into a university you have to pass or be exempted from a matriculation examination. Most universities do not have a matriculation examination of their own but rely entirely on the results of the G.C.E. – Oxford and Cambridge recognize the G.C.E. as giving exemption from matriculation. In general, the universities' minimum entrance requirements are five or six O levels and two A levels. Satisfying the minimum entrance requirements, however, does not carry with it the right of entry to any particular university: it is only a general prerequisite. Competition for university places means that individual universities in practice have plenty of people with more than the minimum requirements to choose from. Particular faculties or departments may insist on a certain standard in their own or other subjects. At Oxford and Cambridge, the prospective student must apply to a particular college and pass the entrance examination of that college. The requirements are listed in *A Compendium of University Entrance Requirements* published by the Committee of Vice-Chancellors. The 1971–2 issue, price 90p, is obtainable from Percy Lund, Humphries and Co. Ltd, The Country Press, Priestman Street, Bradford BD8 8BT.

If a sixth-former wants to go to university, he should apply through the Universities Central Council on Admissions, G.P.O. Box 28, Cheltenham, Glos. Head teachers have all the details. Universities will normally either reject a candidate or accept him subject to a specified performance in the forthcoming A level, and will make their final decision in August.

THE CERTIFICATE OF SECONDARY EDUCATION

Until the summer of 1965 the G.C.E. was the major examination for 16-year-olds. In that year it was joined by a new one, the Certificate of Secondary Education. This was introduced after a good deal of argument, because there were large numbers of teachers, particularly in secondary modern schools, who opposed another external examination. They thought that this would inhibit the better work done in those schools, making it too formal, academic, inflexible and stereotyped. On the other hand there was a growing demand, from pupils, parents and employers, for a nationally recognized qualification. Other teachers argued the need for an incentive in their schools and hoped that the new certificate might offer another route to further education.

The C.S.E. as it was introduced went a long way to meet likely objections. Unlike the G.C.E., it is substantially run by teachers. The governing councils, examinations committees, and subject panels of the fourteen regional examining bodies all have a majority of teachers from the schools affected by the examination. And the three modes of the examination offer a choice of initiatives to teachers. In the first mode, schools submit candidates for the regional examining boards' examinations; in the second, schools or groups of schools put up their own examination schemes for approval by the examining boards; in the third the examinations are set and marked internally by individual schools or groups of schools, and moderated by the boards. It is the third mode, of course, which gives the teachers most freedom – though to the pupils it still offers a nationally recognized examination.

Like the G.C.E. the C.S.E. is a subject examination: a pupil may get a certificate with only one subject on it, and there is no limit to the number of subjects he may take. There are C.S.E. papers in the same sort of academic subjects as are in the G.C.E. but there are others too, like building and engineering science, civics, and typewriting.

There is no pass or fail line. Results are given for each subject in five grades (1 to 5) or are ungraded. Grade 1 indicates a standard comparable with a pass at G.C.E. O level. Grade 4 indicates a standard expected of a 16-year-old of average ability who has followed an appropriate course in the subject. (Grades 2 and 3, not surprisingly, mark standards between these two.) Grade 5 indicates a standard high enough to suggest that it was right for the pupil to enter the examination, but not high enough to get a grade 4. Candidates who do not qualify for grade 5 are ungraded. A pupil can get a certificate for anything more than one grade between 1 and 4. If he gets only one or more grade 5 he does not get a certificate; though where certificates *are* awarded they also record any grade 5. All candidates are told about all their results, including ungradings, but these notices are not the same as a certificate.

The C.S.E. is designed for candidates whose ability overlaps that of pupils taking G.C.E. O level. The latter are held to comprise about one in five of an age-group, and C.S.E. is for the next two in five: from those capable of O level at one end to those just below average in ability at the other. In the summer of 1966, 137,608 pupils entered for the examination offering between them 38 different subjects. There were 520,679 entries in all, 453,972 by mode one, 18,663 by mode two, and 48,044 by mode three. Of the total entries, 14 per cent gained grade 1, 83 per cent grade 4 or better, and 94 per cent grade 5 or better. Only 6 per cent were ungraded. Well over half the candidates came from secondary modern schools. The most popular subjects were English and mathematics (95,000 and 86,000 respectively) and the least popular were Latin, Welsh and Italian.

The Papers

Because of the different modes of the examination, C.S.E. papers vary widely. Many have 'multiple answer' questions in which candidates have to tick or write 'true' or 'false', 'yes' or 'no' to one of four or five possible choices. Here are some examples taken from one examination of the Metropolitan Regional Examinations Board, and they are quoted with the Board's kind permission.

Commerce II: A small firm, owned by a friend of your family, has recently become involved in the export market. The General Manager wishes to show some of the firm's goods in a big Trade Fair to be held in a European capital city. How and where would he set about finding all the information he needs?

Needlecraft, Dress: The pattern for a sleeveless shift dress in your size is $4\frac{1}{2}$ inches longer than you wish to wear it. Write down your bust measurement and pattern size and state how much less of 36 inch material you would need to buy to make the dress economically.

English Paper I: Choose ONE of the following and use it as the starting point for whatever occurs to you – a story, a poem, thoughts, or impressions, your opinions, or a short play.

1. 'That was the time of the sun.'
2. Grown-ups don't care what you do so long as they don't know about it.
3. Every Wednesday afternoon we have compulsory organized games.
4. 'You can get that out of my house just as soon as you like', said my mother.

History: *Either* (a) In the history of Chartism the following facts are important. Write a *few* lines about *three* of them:

 (i) The London Working Men's Association

 (ii) The six points of the Charter

 (iii) Chartist petitions

 (iv) The Chartist Convention, 1839

 (v) The Newport Rising, November 1839

EXAMINATIONS

(vi) The Kennington Common Meeting, 1848

Then say what William Lovett and Feargus O'Connor did for the movement, explaining the differences between them.

Or (b) Answer *both* parts:

What groups joined to form the Labour Representation Committee (Labour party) in 1900?

Describe the part played in the growth of the Labour Party by *two* of the following:

(i) Keir Hardie

(ii) Sidney and Beatrice Webb

(iii) Ramsay MacDonald

(iv) Clement Attlee

Geography: (1) From Britain's neighbours, name and locate an example of a delta, a fiord, and a U-shaped valley.

2. For each, describe (i) its scenery and (ii) how it is used by people. Illustrate your answer with diagrams or sketch maps.

German Paper II: Write *in German* a composition of about 120 *words* on *one* of the following subjects:

1. Wie ich das Wochenende verbringe.

2. Dankesbrief an einen Freund (eine Freundin) nach 3 Wochen Ferien in Deutschland.

3. Write in German the story which the pictures (on the opposite page) suggest to you.

Social Studies: Give some arguments both for and against the introduction of compulsory comprehensive schools for the whole of British secondary education.

Mathematics Paper I: In this question numbers are written in various scales: the particular scale used for each number is indicated in brackets. Where no scale is shown the number is written in the scale of 10. For example, $121_{(3)}$ is 121 in the scale of 3 and $121_{(3)} = 16$. (The candidate is asked to write 'true' or 'false' against each question):

(i) $10001_{(2)} = 17$ (ii) $123_{(4)} = 27$ (iii) $3130_{(5)} = 320_{(6)}$

(iv) $12300_{(5)}$ is exactly divisible by 25

(v) $12300_{(6)}$ is exactly divisible by 25

THE PAPERS

Science Paper II, Biology: Write short notes on *four* of the following:

1. *Viruses.* (What are they? Why was it a long time before they were discovered? How can people be protected against them?)
2. *Mammals.* (What are they? Name three special features. Name three mammals.)
3. *Immunity.* (What is it? Difference between active and passive immunity? How can it be acquired?)
4. *Muscles.* (Name three types. Where are they found? What can all muscles do?)
5. *Fossils.* (What are they? Describe one way by which they are found. What can man discover from them?)
6. *Blood Vessels.* (Name the three types and describe them. What function have they in common and how do they differ in function?)

Building Studies Paper I, Technology and Design: 1. Describe the method you would adopt to keep a cavity wall clear of mortar droppings and how you would clear mortar from the cavity on the completion of the walls. Explain the purpose of keeping the cavity clear. How and at what distances horizontally and vertically are the two leaves of the cavity tied together? Illustrate your answer with sketches.

2. When designing the layout of the pipes for supplying cold water to a bungalow, what points should be borne in mind? Draw a typical layout for the cold water services for the bungalow.

3. The casement windows for a bungalow have been delivered to a site without any protective timber treatment. The timber appears rather knotty and resinous. Describe the preparation for painting necessary before the windows are fixed in position. Give your reasons for the treatment. Then continue to describe the operations necessary to bring the casement windows to a full gloss finish.

CHAPTER SIX

Choice – and Fee-paying

PARENTAL CHOICE IN THE STATE SYSTEM

PARENTS are frequently confused about their right to choose one state school rather than another. There is a still popular belief that head teachers have the power to admit or to reject. There is also a growing belief that the 1944 Act gives parents an unqualified right to choose the school to which their child should go. Both of these beliefs are wrong.

Let us see first what the 1944 Act actually says. The relevant section is Section 76.

> 76. *Pupils to be educated in accordance with wishes of parents*
> In the exercise and performance of all powers and duties conferred and imposed on them by this Act the Minister and local education authorities shall have regard to the general principle that, so far as is compatible with the provision of efficient instruction and training and the avoidance of unreasonable public expenditure, pupils are to be educated in accordance with the wishes of their parents.

Let us see now what Section 76 *does not* say. It does not say that pupils must be educated in accordance with the wishes of their parents. Neither does it say that the local authority must follow the principle that they should be so educated. What it does is to lay down a general principle to which the local authority must have regard. The authority can, of course, have regard to other things as well and can also make exceptions to the general principle if it wants to. However, if a local authority were to direct a child to attend a particular school it would be almost impossible to prove that the authority had not at some point 'had regard' to the general principle.

There are also two hefty qualifications in Section 76. They are 'so far as is compatible with the provision of efficient instruction and training and the avoidance of unreasonable public expenditure'. In practice this means, for example, that if your son is not selected for a grammar school place you have no right under

Section 76 to demand one – though you can always try to produce evidence that the selection was mistaken. Equally if your daughter is 5 you cannot insist that she goes to a nearby school for the over-7s even if the nearest school for 5-year-olds is a mile away. The qualification that unreasonable public expenditure must be avoided means, for example, that you cannot force your local authority to allow your son to go to an expensive boarding school nor insist that your daughter goes to your wife's old school which happens to be miles away in another county.

Parents might well wonder if they have any right of choice left. The answer is that they have, and the Department of Education has issued a *Manual of Guidance* on the subject. The manual says that it simply sets out 'some of the relevant considerations which may need to be balanced against each other before a decision is reached'. In practice, however, these 'considerations' have come to be accepted as reasonable grounds for choosing one school rather than another. They are as follows:

1. *Religion* Denominational feelings are one of the commonest and strongest reasons for choosing an alternative school and most authorities recognize this. It is not generally known, however, that a parent need not show that he belongs to any specific religious denomination. A man may be an ardent Methodist but if he wants his child brought up as a Roman Catholic he cannot be told he has no right to select a Roman Catholic school. Naturally a parent's own religious practice will be taken into account in judging the seriousness of his request. For example, the ardent Methodist might want his daughter to go to a convent school for other than religious reasons, say the indefinable social tone it imparts.

2. *Languages* In Wales some parents are very anxious that their children should be taught in one language rather than another. The Department recognizes that it would be reasonable for authorities to organize schools so that they can meet a demand for instruction in either English or Welsh and that where a parent can choose it is reasonable for him to do so.

3. *Convenience* Another common reason for choosing an alter-

native school is the presence of traffic dangers. Parents can also urge that their child should go to the same school as an elder brother or sister so that he might be escorted safely. Normally a parent will want to choose a nearby school rather than one farther away.

4. *Medical* If it could be shown to be desirable that a child should attend one school rather than another on medical grounds, the parents' wish would almost certainly be upheld. Much can be done with a doctor's certificate.

5. *Special facilities* Where both parents go out to work the Department says it would be reasonable for their children to attend schools where they can have a midday meal if this were practicable.

6. *Family associations* The Department is sympathetic to old boy and old girl feelings.

7. *Co-education* The desire to choose either a single-sex school or a co-educational school is normally recognized as reasonable.

8. *Advanced work* In a small number of cases a parent might choose one secondary school rather than another on the ground that the first provides a particular type of advanced work and the second does not.

These are the grounds on which parents may seek to choose one school rather than another. The main reason why a local authority might refuse a parent's request is that they have some 'zoning' plan for local schools. In many areas the provision of efficient instruction involves allocating 'catchment areas' to each school so as to avoid overcrowding in some and empty classrooms in others. The *Manual of Guidance* gives the authorities their cue when it says that it would not be compatible with the provision of efficient instruction and training if the schools of the parent's choice (or the class which the child would enter) were full. The manual recognizes that it may be necessary under a zoning scheme for some children to attend a school other than that nearest to their homes. But the Secretary of State does assume that local authorites will zone only where necessary, will stop doing so when the need for it is past, and will take traffic dangers, denominational preferences, and exceptional cases into account. When a zoning scheme is first introduced children should normally be allowed to stay in the schools to which they have previously been going and in any case the authorities should publicize their intention by circular letters to parents, parents' meetings, announcements in the papers and so on.

These, then, are the limits and possibilities of parental choice. What happens if a parent chooses a school and the school or the local authority will not agree? Can a parent insist on his right of choice and make it effective? Happily, the need to appeal and insist seldom arises. Most local education authorities are willing within reasonable limits to meet parent's wishes. But occasionally a parent is worried or annoyed because what seem to him quite legitimate reasons for preferring one school to another are brushed aside, and the authority in a dictatorial and bureaucratic manner arbitrarily reject his choice and insist that the child attends a particular school. The first thing he can do is to make quite certain he has exhausted all the normal processes of local government. He should seek a personal interview with the education officer invoking the help of his local councillor if necessary. He should also appeal to the education committee. If this fails, his only recourse is a complicated procedure which can be unpleasant and harmful to his child. The procedure is set out here, but no one would recommend parents to follow it unless they are in dire extremities.

The parent's first step is to appeal to the Secretary of State. He can do this directly or through his local Member of Parliament. There is no particular advantage in going through an M.P. except that M.P.s are much more practised than parents in writing to Ministers. There is no backstairs pressure an M.P. can bring to bear. The parent's appeal can be on two grounds. He can complain under Section 68 of the 1944 Act that the authority are acting unreasonably, and under Section 99 that the authority are failing in their duty under Section 76. As already explained, Section 76 is hedged about with qualifications and it is impossible to show that the authority have not 'had regard to' the parent's wishes even if they reject them. More crucial perhaps is the fact that the Secretary of State has normally refused to act against an authority under Section 68.

To explain what a parent can do if he feels the authority are acting unreasonably and has failed to convince the Minister of this we shall have to start with the duties which the 1944 Act lays on the parents and on the authorities. The final responsibility for seeing that the child receives education falls clearly upon the parent. In education law in this country it is the duty of the parent of every child of compulsory school age to cause him to receive full-time education suitable to his age, ability and aptitude. This can be done either by full-time attendance at school or in some other way. But the responsibility and duty is with the parent. The authorities have different duties. They are responsible for seeing that there are sufficient suitable schools and for bringing the parent to court if he fails in *his* duty.

The parent may fail in several ways. He may refuse to send the child to school at all and not provide any alternative education; he may send the child only very occasionally or for only part of the day; he may send the child to the school he chooses, knowing full well that the child will not be admitted. If he keeps the child at home he may offer only part-time or otherwise unsuitable education. Whatever he does, as soon as it appears to the authority that the parent is failing in his duty, the authority have an obligation to act. The parent might even say, 'Look, I'm failing in my duty, now you must act.'

What happens then? The authority must serve upon the parent a notice, requiring him within a specified time, not less than fourteen days from the service of the notice, to satisfy them that the child is receiving full-time education suitable to his age, ability and aptitude, either by regular attendance or otherwise. The authority have no option in the matter. If the child is not receiving education, the notice must be served.

Serving a notice does not take us very far by itself. But it can be a beginning of the complicated process by which a parent can insist on his right of choice. Suppose that, instead of sending the child to the school the authority have chosen, the parent just ignores the notice and either keeps the child at home unsuitably educated or sends him daily to a school where he is daily refused admission. What then? At this stage the authority can serve a written notice of their intention to make a School Attendance Order for the child. The Order cannot be made until fifteen days after this written notice has been sent. It is at this point that the law gives the parent an opportunity of nominating the school he wishes the child to attend. The Act says that between the notice of the Order and the issue of the Order itself, the parent can select a school at which he desires the child to become a registered pupil, and that school will, unless the Secretary of State otherwise directs, be named in the Order.

This is reflected in the terms of the notice to the parents, the first part of which is:

1. I am directed by the X local education authority to refer to the notice addressed to you on the X date, and to state that the authority are of the opinion that your child is not receiving efficient full-time education suitable to his age, ability and aptitude, and that it is expedient that the child should attend school.
2. The authority therefore propose to serve upon you, under the provisions of Section 37(2) of the Education Act 1944, a School Attendance Order which will require you to cause the child to become a registered pupil at a particular school to be named in the Order. If you fail to comply with the Order you will be guilty of an offence and it will be the duty of the authority to take proceedings against you.
3. You have the right under Section 37 of the Act to select the school at which you want your child to attend. It is therefore open to you at any time up to fifteen days from the date of this letter to notify the authority of the name of the school which you want your child to attend.

That is not quite all the letter – but before finishing it let us look again at the Act. Suppose the authority do not like the school the parent has chosen, what can they do about it? Well, the Act says (and the precise words are important) that if they are of the opinion that the school selected by the parent as the school to be named in a School Attendance Order is unsuitable to the age, ability or aptitude of the child, or that attendance at the school so selected would involve unreasonable expense to the authority, the authority may, after giving the parent notice of their intention to do so, apply to the Secretary of State for a direction determining what school is to be named in the Order. It is extremely important to notice that the authority cannot go to the Secretary of State just because they do not like the school chosen by the parent. They have to show that the choice is unsuitable, or would cause unreasonable expense.

Now we can go back and complete the letter to the parent.

4. The authority consider the following school (or schools) suitable for your child. If you select this school (or one of these schools) this will be the school named in the Order. If you would prefer some other school you may indicate its name, but the authority will then have to consider whether the school chosen by you is suitable and also, in cases where this question arises, whether unreasonable expense would be involved. If they are not satisfied they may decide to refer the matter to the Secretary of State for Education and Science, who has the power to direct what school shall be named in the Order.
5. If you do not choose any school or do not reply to this letter within fifteen days of the date of despatch, the authority will proceed to make an Order inserting the name of X school.

The parent has a specific right to nominate the school. The authority can appeal to the Secretary of State but only after telling the parent that they propose to do so and only on the grounds of unsuitability and unreasonable cost. The Secretary of State has the final word as to what school is stated in the Order. If after all this the parent still refuses to send the child to the school named in the Order, the case can be taken to the courts, since it is an offence to fail to comply with the terms of the School Attendance Order. The parent can try to bring before the courts the whole of the facts and circumstances. If the courts acquitted the parent they could order that the School Attendance Order should cease to be in force – and we are back where we started.

The process outlined here is long and difficult: it is almost a war of attrition. It might almost have been designed to be as difficult as possible, and certainly very few parents have tried to use it. But it has its advantages. It is the only way at present in which a parent has a legal right to nominate the school of his choice. If he uses it, only the Secretary of State, not the local authority, can gainsay him. A parent who followed the procedure step by step would be in a much stronger position than one who simply wrote to his M.P. or direct to the Secretary of State. The length of the process need not be to the parent's disadvantage always. Sometimes the mere threat to embark upon it will persuade the authority to agree with the parent's wishes. Its great disadvantage is that the child is made a pawn in the game. He has to be kept at home, or taken daily to a school which daily refuses him admission, while the process works itself out. And it can be used only when a child starts at a new primary or secondary school. If a child is already on the register of a school, he cannot be removed without the consent of the authority. If he is then kept at home, the authority can simply prosecute without the attendance order procedure.

Keeping the Child at Home

There is one final point. What if a parent wishes his child not to go to school at all? The 1944 Act says that it is the duty of the parent to see that the child gets efficient full-time education suitable to his age, ability and aptitude, 'either by regular attendance at school or otherwise'. There is not very much guidance as to what kind of 'otherwise' is acceptable. The only obvious case under the present law is that of Mrs Joy Baker, who fought the Norfolk County Council for eight years for the right not to send her children to school. In the course of this she was fined and sentenced to imprisonment (which she avoided on appeal) and had to fight the county's attempt to make her children wards of court. The basis of her case was that she disapproved of schools and that her children could be seen to be 'educated' – even though they received no formal instruction. She herself had no special training to be a teacher and encouraged the children to follow their own interests. The moral of this seems to be that you can keep your children at home all the time and refuse to send them to school provided you are prepared to fight it out with the authorities for eight years.

CHOICE – AND FEE-PAYING

CHOICE AMONG INDEPENDENT SCHOOLS

By contrast with the state system the possibility of choice of independent schools is enormous. It is true that there are some particular schools which are very difficult to get into, so a parent may be denied his particular choice. Equally there are some particular children for whom finding a suitable school may be a very great problem. Even so, a parent who wants his child to go to a traditional public school can normally expect to get him into one, and the same applies to the rather smaller number of parents who want 'progressive' or 'freedom' schools. What they have to do is pay for it. Even here, as can be seen later, there are ways of avoiding shouldering the burden of heavy fees all at once.

The point is that a parent with money who starts to consider schools is not bound in any way by the area in which he lives or by the particular schools that happen to be available locally. He can look round the whole country. He can favour any kind of school. And if he finds after two or three years that the school of his choice is not what he thought, he can take his child away and choose somewhere else. There are all kinds of reasons why people decide to pay for their children's education. They include habit, snobbery, ignorance, social aspiration, a belief in boarding education, relatively small classes or the career advantages of the old boy net. It remains true that the most distinctive difference in practice between people who pay privately and people who don't is that people who pay choose.

HOW TO JUDGE A SCHOOL

In general it is the people who pay fees who choose. They at any rate expect to do so and may have had some practice in it, especially if their family have been doing it for ages (though this often means simply 'choosing' the same school generation after generation). People whose children go to state schools may not have very much choice – but they occasionally have some. They too need to know how to choose wisely if they get the chance. And it would be no bad thing if parents approached the state schools to which their children had been allocated *as if* they had a choice. If they have none, there is all the more reason for looking at the school carefully and critically, discovering what it sets out to do, what it offers and what it lacks. This will enable parents to support or supplement what the school is doing. A bit of informed inquiry does no school any harm, and one way of increasing the chance of choice among state schools is to show that parents want it and can use it wisely when they get it. This section, therefore, is about how to judge a school – any school.

No one can tell you what school to choose. Choosing a school is a question of matching two uniques – a child and a school – and it can be done only by someone with an intimate knowledge of both. Parents at any rate have the chance to know their own child well, at least from one point of view. They can try to know him better by hearing what other adults (say teachers) have to say about him, having him tested intellectually or psychologically or by accepting the results of school or public examinations. All these things can widen a parent's knowledge and reduce his bias towards his child.

It is nowhere near so simple to gain intimate knowledge of a school. Most parents rely pretty heavily on hearsay, and this can be very unreliable. The fact that six of your friends say that school A is a good one is no guarantee that it will be all right for your child. Probably their opinion is based on a combination of rumour, a quick general impression and the absence of obvious disaster or unhappiness. Hearsay evidence from people engaged in education is perhaps a bit better, though it is very surprising how little teachers know of other teachers' schools. A school is a very closed world. Even inspectors doing a full inspection lasting several days do not see the school as it works normally, and inspectors' reports are anyway entirely confidential. You may feel that you can judge by 'results' – though even here parents are often undecided as to whether the most important result is the 'type of child' a school produces or its success in the relevant examinations or on the sports field. Many parents quickly become proud of whatever the school does – whatever their expectations had been initially.

Some fee-paying parents go to advisory bodies or scholastic

agencies. These are useful in so far as they can give factual information or have an up-to-date note of vacancies, but they cannot choose a school for your child any more than anyone else can.

The obvious thing to do is to see the schools themselves. Ring up or write to the head and fix an appointment – in state or independent schools. You cannot choose a school in any real sense unless you visit it. The more schools you visit, of course, the better will be your standards of comparison. Even so it is easy to be misled. Many parents regress to their own childhood when they get anywhere near a school and find themselves overawed by a headmaster who would not be so impressive if they met him casually. The golden rule is to start from the child. This may seem merely platitudinous, but there are a large number of people who do not do it. The father who put his son's name down at birth for his own old school is not making a choice at all but giving way to a conditioned reflex. What you have to do is to decide, as near the relevant time as is practicable, what sort of things your child needs and wants. You can then make a list of the things you consider important and against this you can judge the available alternatives. Every parent's list will be somewhat different, if only in its order of priorities. But every parent should try to make his own list formally or informally and taking the best advice, both from friends and professionally, that he can get. The following are examples of some of the things parents should consider. They are not meant to be an exhaustive list but simply a guide. And when all is done there is perhaps no way of judging the final quality of a school – you can only guess at it from the way in which it measures up to the individual demands you make of it.

Type of School What kind of school are you looking for, or visiting? Is it a state, direct grant, independent school? How many children are there? – boys or girls or mixed? To what age do children normally stay there? Is it a day or boarding school? Some children need a boarding school, and for many different reasons: the most obvious is that the family itself is in some way incomplete. You might also feel that boarding schools have positive advantages (see pages 163–9).

HOW TO JUDGE A SCHOOL

Curriculum and Methods What is taught differs considerably between state and independent primary schools and between individual secondary schools. To what subjects do you attach greatest importance? What range and level of subjects does a secondary school offer? Does a primary school offer music? Methods differ too, particularly in primary schools. Do you want an education based on what is known about children's development or a régime of more formal instruction?

Attitude to Parents Does the school welcome parents, not only on formal occasions and for fund-raising, but at other times? Is it easy to get to see the head and other teachers? You will be lucky if your child goes through school entirely without problems: can these be settled in the normal course of events, or does it involve formal arrangements? Does the school treat you like a human being?

Fees If it is a fee-paying school, you will want to know what the fees are, and if there are any extras. Is there any way of getting help to pay them, either through scholarships offered by the school or through your local authority? Even in state schools you may be asked to buy a special uniform or sports equipment.

Entrance How is entrance to the school arranged? Find out about examinations, if any, and when a child has to be entered. In fee-paying schools it is as well to discover whether 'putting a boy's name down' means anything at all.

Buildings and Grounds It is possible to get a good education in a building which is very nearly a slum, but it is obviously worth considering the age, state of repair and adequacy of the school buildings. Are they overcrowded? Does the school find it difficult to give all children some time in a laboratory? Are there classes going on in the corridors? Are there any playing fields, and if so, where? In boarding schools, are the dormitories civilized – or do the children have study-bedrooms?

Staff How many teachers are there, compared with the number of pupils? Are there both men and women? Are they capable of offering as a body pretty well any subject your child might want to study? Are they all very old – or very young? How often do they change?

Academic Standards The only rule of thumb there is for academic standards is some sort of external examination. What sort of performance does the school put up at 11+ or in G.C.E. and entrance exams for universities? In secondary schools, discover to what age pupils normally stay there. If a prospectus refers vaguely to 'several awards at universities', make the headmaster be specific about how many and where.

Out-of-School Activities In any good school there will be quite a lot going on outside the formal lessons. You can discover how much and what. Are there music, drama and clubs and societies of all kinds? Is there a cadet force (compulsory?), scouts or guides?

Sport What emphasis is placed on sport? How many times a week will a child have compulsory games? Is the emphasis on team games, or are there particular sports or physical activity in which the school specializes? Is it possible to learn to swim?

Other Children Many parents are concerned only to preserve (or improve) their children's accents, but others think it important for a school to be socially or intellectually homogeneous or diverse.

Punishment and Discipline Most schools have some form of prefect system. You can discover how the prefects are selected and whether, in boarding schools, there is any fagging. What punishments are used – and, more important perhaps, by whom?

Miscellaneous There are some questions to which even headmasters normally cannot give accurate answers but which are very important to a child. How much bullying goes on in a school? Are homosexual activities common? These are more crucial questions in boarding schools, perhaps, but you need to consider them in day schools. The most you can hope to do is decide whether you think a bit of bullying, beating or homosexuality is of any consequence.

Religion and Co-education There are two very important questions which you may want to decide as a parent but which it is very difficult to decide from studying your particular child. These are religion and co-education. At the age when one normally chooses a school for a child you cannot tell whether he personally will thrive in a religious or non-religious, in a co-educational or a single-sexed school. You can only go on general principles and your own prejudices. Most religious parents will want their children to go to religious schools, but even non-religious parents might want to choose a particular kind of religious background. It is worth discovering how much religious observance is compulsory. In particular, parents of some faiths should discover early whether their children might be excluded on religious grounds.

Conclusion These then are some of the things which are useful to have in mind when judging a school. People who pay tend to consider them anyway, though perhaps not as thoroughly as they should. People whose children go to state schools may not have very much choice. But they may have some, and they should take as much care as they can in judging what is available.

PAYING FOR EDUCATION

Most people who work pay for education whether they have children or not. They pay in rates and taxes. If you want to know how much we all pay in this way in your area, have a look at the back of your rate demand note. No education in this country is 'free', but in the state service people contribute according to their means and not according to the number of children they have. And even in the state service people can pay for the 'extras' of education individually. Simply keeping a child at school, especially when he might otherwise be earning, is an expense, and so are any books or instruments like slide rules, violins or cricket bats. Some parents may want their children to have more tuition than the state schools provide. They may do this by private coaching or by taking out a correspondence course. They may buy an expensive encyclopedia.

CHOICE – AND FEE-PAYING

To a limited extent, people can get help with some of these added expenses. The most obvious way is through maintenance grants which the local education authorities are empowered to make to the parents of needy children. Some counties have schemes of help specially for buying school uniforms. There is no consistency in this at all. In some local authorities a child over 15 may get a very generous maintenance grant. In others he may get nothing at all. In a sense the whole of the school meals and milk service is a contribution towards maintenance of children at school. The milk is free in infant schools and the price of school meals does not cover the whole cost of providing them. Family allowances are another maintenance contribution.

It is people whose children go to independent schools who are normally thought of as paying for education. A public school can cost £700 a year in fees alone and most people expect their sons at any rate to stay at one for five years – making £3,500 in all. Then one has to add to this the cost of keep, feeding and clothing the boy, buying school uniform, sports equipment and so on. Obviously many people look round for ways of easing this financial burden.

Some wonder whether anything can be done through the local authority. This is unlikely in most cases. You have to show that there are special circumstances, like the death or separation of parents; the parent's need to travel a great deal, particularly abroad; a doctor's statement that boarding school is medically or psychologically necessary (this is difficult to establish); or a clear demonstration that a child cannot get a suitable education except at a boarding school. If you establish one of these grounds, the local authority will offer you a place in one of their own boarding schools – if they have one. If not, they may offer you a place provided by another local authority – and it is only failing this that the authority will consider paying fees on your behalf at an independent boarding school.

If your child goes to a local authority boarding school there will be no tuition fees but you will have to pay according to your means for the child's maintenance and you will have to supply his clothes and keep him during the holidays. The full maintenance fee at local authority boarding schools is usually between

£280 and £320 a year. A very few authorities will pay the tuition fees of pupils at public schools as a hang-over from the 1930s, when it was thought that selected children of poor parents should go to public schools.

When a child gets a grammar school place at 11+ his parents sometimes think of sending him to a local boarding school, getting the local authority to pay tuition fees on the strength of the 11+ success and making up the difference themselves. Although it would be too sweeping to say that this never happens, local authorities will normally not pay for a place in someone else's school if they have a similar school themselves. They regard it, understandably enough, as 'unreasonable public expenditure'.

A popular alternative to both claiming help from the local education authorities on grounds of need and actually paying the full fees of an independent school is to get the child in to a direct grant grammar school. As has been shown on page 103 the fees are considerably lower than those of independent schools, even for boarding places. There is in fact an imperfectly concealed state subsidy. The trouble here is that you have to show that your child is at least of grammar school standard – and there are not all that number of boarding places in direct grant schools (something over 9,000, in fact).

Many parents imagine that their children might win scholarships to public schools. There are scholarships going, but not all that many. The typical boys' public school has two or three. And a scholarship rarely covers the cost of school fees. Many are for £50 or £100 a year, which is a help, but it is not normally enough. The luckiest poor are those who are favoured by past donors: for some reason the clergy, schoolmasters and warriors have numbers of scholarships dedicated to their children. A glance through the *Public Schools' Year Book* will give you an idea of what is going.

For most parents the only way to meet heavy school fees is to be able to afford it! All the expedients tend to depend on your having quite a lot of money anyway, or on getting someone else, with money, to pay for you. For example, some parents can get fees paid by a child's grandparents or from the father's firm. Before 1968, anyone except a parent could pay for a child's education through deeds of covenant of settlements. This method was comparatively cheap because of the income tax remissions obtained, though if enough was paid to bring a child's income to more than £100 a year the parents lost the child allowance. After the Finance Act of 1968 any income of minors counted as parental income for tax purposes, so the advantages of this method disappeared. Most fees were met, normally out of capital, in this way, so the the effect of the change on numbers going to independent schools would have been interesting – except that the change was being reversed as this book was being revised.

A remaining way of easing the burden is simply by saving in some way. You can pay a lump sum in advance to cover the normal five year period a child stays at school and there are insurance agencies which will make provision for this even if you have not decided which particular school you want. The leading public schools have arrangements whereby a single composition fee can be paid well in advance. The advantage is that the lump sum is less than five times the current fee: the disadvantage is that it does not cover the real possibility of the fees rising even before the child goes to the school. The terms offered are not particularly attractive, except in those schools which allow for rising fees. You would probably do better by investing a lump sum. You can also, in a similar way, provide a rising amount of money throughout the five years of school life for an initial capital outlay of less than the composition fee. What you need for all this is a friendly stockbroker or accountant.

Yet another method is to take out an endowment policy immediately on the birth of the child. Any insurance broker will explain this. There is a genial variation on this theme. On the birth of the child you take out a twenty-one-year endowment policy with profits. You pay the premiums regularly for thirteen years. From then on you borrow on the strength of the policy the premium, the fees you have to pay and the interest on the loan! The burden of fees is entirely removed, you have very useful life cover, and the 'with profits' clause assures you of a handsome cash profit as well.

CHAPTER SEVEN

Medical and Other Special Services

THE duty of the local authorities under the Education Act, 1944 to contribute towards the physical development of the community – as well as the spiritual, moral, and mental development – is a wide one. They have to create conditions for healthy growth and encourage their pupils towards healthy living. They must provide light, spacious, clean, well-ventilated, and well-heated schools with adequate playing space, gymnasia, swimming baths, proper lavatories, and possibly school camps in the country. They can be the means of providing playing fields.

Meals and Milk

More specifically, however, they have a duty to provide 'milk, meals, and other refreshments' for pupils in their schools. The Building Regulations lay down the amount of dining space that is required to be made for every child expected to take meals, and the Provision of Meals Regulations require the authorities to employ school meals organizers and adequate kitchen staffs. Up to 1968 they could also require a teacher to supervise his own pupils at meals unless the authority concerned thought this would adversely affect the quality of the teaching. After that date, and following a campaign by the National Union of Teachers, these supervisory duties were accepted as voluntary, causing difficulties in a few schools.

Milk – a third of a pint a day – is provided free in all infant schools. Milk in secondary schools was withdrawn in September 1968 as part of the Government's economy measures. Free milk for children over 7 was withdrawn in the summer of 1971, also as an economy, but local authorities were empowered to sell milk to older children, including those in secondary schools. Older primary school pupils may get free milk by producing a doctor's certificate. For meals parents are charged a proportion of the cost. The charge may be wholly or partially remitted in cases of need. The cost of school meals and milk, borne initially by the local authorities, is partly met by the rate support grant, like other items of local authority expenditure. The local authorities can make arrangements to provide milk and meals for independent schools in their area.

In the autumn of 1969 over five million pupils were eating school dinners in state schools – 70 per cent of the total numbers. Only a few schools or departments out of the total of 30,000 had no school meals facilities. Probably nine out of every ten primary school children take milk at school (including independent schools).

Clothing and Cleansing

The local authorities also have power to provide children with clothing to ensure that they are sufficiently and suitably clad. They must, however, require the parent to pay as much as they think he can without financial hardship. Equally the local authorities can see that any pupil is not verminous and foul. After an inspection the authorities can order the pupil concerned to be cleansed and if the child again becomes verminous or foul the parent is liable to a fine of one pound. In 1967 over 200,000 children were found to be infested, and the parents of 32,000 of these were given notice to cleanse them. 6,524 individual pupils were served with cleansing orders under Section 54(3) of the Education Act, 1944, but it is not known how many of these were satisfactorily cleansed by the parent and how many were cleansed by the local education authority.

Medical and Dental Inspections

Finally, the local education authorities have to arrange for the medical inspection of children at appropriate intervals in all schools which they maintain, and they may require pupils to be submitted for these inspections. It is their duty to provide free medical and dental treatment for pupils at their schools. Normally treatment is given under the National Health Service, though the school health service must continue to offer dental treatment or arrange for it to be given in hospital. The general pattern of medical inspections for schoolchildren is that all the children of an age-group are examined on their entry to primary school, just before they leave school at 15, and once or twice in between. Recently a number of authorities have been giving up the intermediate examination for all children and examining instead only selected children who seem to need it. Every local education authority must appoint a principal school medical officer and a principal school dental officer.

In 1969 over 1¾ million children were given routine medical inspections (15 per cent of them were found to need treatment), and 1¼ million had special inspections and re-inspections. Some 434,000 were treated for defective vision and squint, and 104,000 for defects of ear, nose, and throat. Some 3,000 hearing aids were provided, and spectacles were prescribed for under ¼ million children. Over 300,000 minor ailments were treated. Some 82,000 pupils were given speech therapy and 66,000 child guidance treatment. Nearly 4½ million had their teeth inspected. Nearly 2½ million were found to require treatment, and over 1¼ million were actually treated.

It is difficult to say precisely what the staff of the school health service amounts to, as so many of them devote only part of their time to the service. There were in 1969, for example, 3,204 medical officers, but the full-time equivalent of this number is reckoned as only 880. The full-time equivalent of other officers is: dental officers 1,422; dental surgery assistants, 1,651; school nurses, 3,334; and 239 nursing assistants. The service also employed the full-time equivalents of 170 physiotherapists, 20 chiropodists, 140 psychiatrists, over 400 educational psychologists and over 200 psychiatric social workers.

CHAPTER EIGHT

Educational Controversies

EDUCATION as a subject creates quite a bit of disagreement among its practitioners. This is not surprising. It is an intensely personal subject and any attempt to generalize about it is bound to lead to controversy. There are, in fact, a number of running conflicts in education which will probably never be resolved. Which is preferable, co-educational or segregated schooling, boarding schools or day schools? So far as children are concerned as individuals, there is no final answer to these questions. It all depends on the child. Equally, there can be no final answer so far as teachers are concerned. Teachers differ. The best one can do is to say that, so far as one can see, most children or most teachers do best in such and such circumstances. Even then people will not agree on what they mean by 'best'.

Far too little has been done to discover what various theories of education actually mean in practice. Often the necessary long-term and detailed research has not been done. So the arguments can go on and no one need be under any obligation to refer to the facts. In this unsatisfactory situation the best that can be done in a reference book is to state baldly the common arguments used on each side of perennial controversies. It is impossible to comment on their validity.

CO-EDUCATION

The main argument in favour of co-education is that it is 'natural'. Boys and girls exist. They live together in families; later they work together and get married to each other. The place for the sexes to begin learning to live and work together is at school. Good emotional and social relationships depend to a large extent on the background built up from an early age, and segregated schooldays distort the background, making satisfactory relationships difficult later. Bringing boys and girls together in their formative years creates a basis for understanding later: artificial barriers in childhood create problems, especially during adolescence, which are quite unnecessary. Education is not only a matter of learning facts, it is a preparation for life. In co-educational schools the boys and girls learn how to get on with each other. Children from schools with only their own half of the human species are reserved and awkward with the other half. After leaving school they go through a period of quite unnecessary misery and insecurity. Adolescence is bound to be made worse when schools pretend that sex is something that doesn't exist. Indeed, in turning children in upon themselves they risk making sex an obsession or diverting it into homosexual directions.

Other countries adopt co-education as a matter of course and look upon the single-sex system with surprise and even horror. They know that judged by academic standards (a common argument for segregation) co-education works. There is some evidence that it is academically better, especially for girls. Sex segregation in British schools is simply an historical accident, one of the dire results of the influence of public schools. We do not have single-sex families, single-sex parents or single-sex factories – why single-sex schools? It is probably some hangover from the idea that women are not worth educating. Segregation is also harmful because it means that staffs are segregated too. Girls get no chance of being taught by men, or boys by women. And in their work the teachers have colleagues of the same sex only. This accounts for the curious narrowness of single-sex schools. But children learn not only from teachers but from each other. The sexes have different approaches to subjects and in a co-educational school these differences can enrich the lessons. Boys and girls teach each other because they are alive to different levels of meaning. The farce of single-sex education is often most visible in the school play, with the boys playing the parts of wives and mistresses and the girls striding about in Wellington boots and false beards.

The main argument against co-education is that boys and girls differ. They differ in their biological make-up, their interests, their aspirations and expectations. More important, they differ in their rates of development. At 13 girls are gaining maturity, poise and emotional attachments, while boys are still unruly, sissy-scorning toughs. Trying to teach them in the same class is like trying to teach two groups of different ages together. Left to themselves, children naturally choose friends among contemporaries of the same sex.

Adolescents may be reserved and awkward but there is nothing to suggest that this is very much lessened in co-educational schools. Adolescents are confused, aggressive, shy and difficult wherever they are. Indeed co-education simply makes matters worse. The child has to cope both with his school work and the problems of facing an emotional change made obvious by the presence of the opposite sex. The idea that happy marriages are more easily made by people from co-educational schools and that people from single-sex schools have less satisfactory emotional relationships is a myth. The idea that single-sex schools produce homosexuals and lesbians is an old wives' tale.

Single-sex education may be an historical accident and very rare abroad, but it has been proved here by the test of time. People go on doing it because it seems right. There is no reason why schools should copy the pattern of adult society. They differ from adult society in all kinds of respects. They are designed for children, not for adults. They are and should be different from the adult world. What is important is that there should be places where children can best grow and develop. It may be true that teachers in single-sex schools do not have colleagues of the opposite sex. This is equally true of many other jobs, and it does not follow, of course, that they have no contact at all with the opposite sex. Not all teachers are anxious to teach in co-educational schools.

The differences between boys and girls militate against their learning together. Indeed, lessons have to be planned as two at a time because what interests one half bores the other. Single-sex schools are communities where boys or girls can develop best at their own pace. For this, boys playing Lady Macbeth (as they did in Shakespeare's day) is a small price to pay.

BOARDING SCHOOLS

Normally when people argue about boarding schools they think of single-sex institutions, although there are a few co-educational ones. Similarly there are some single-sex boarding schools (those run by the Society of Friends, for example) to which many of the traditional objections do not apply. In general, however, the arguments for and against the traditional single-sex boarding schools are as follows.

The chief arguments for boarding school are that children enjoy it, are better educated and get better character training.

Children enjoy living in large groups and thrive on it. Every boarding-school child is continually conscious of living in a closed and privileged institution. This gives him a real sense of security and of 'belonging': he knows he is an insider. The child who goes to a day school is rootless, a commuter, his day divided firmly into two.

Boarding school is a complete society at work: the day school is only a partial community. Seeing the whole society and being partially responsible for running it in the last years develop a child's self-assurance and his ability to get on with and handle other people. This is why leaders in many fields come from boarding schools even when the schools do not set out to inculcate 'leadership'. The child's knowledge of people is broadened: he is not restricted to making friends in his locality or of his own age. The habit of looking beyond his home locality is built into his upbringing. He gets practice in assessing the qualities of his companions without the interference of parental opinion. Sometimes children need help and do not get it from parents or teachers (both are human and both can fail). Often they can work out their needs among their companions and it is easy to do this in the community of the boarding school. The rough and tumble of life among their contemporaries can be a help as well as the character-building experience it is more often recognized to be.

Most children enjoy and respond to living with their contemporaries in an environment especially designed for them. This advantage is combined with the fact that home ties are not broken. Children spend at least a quarter of the year at home. At school, they are in touch with their parents through visits and letters. They are not, as most opponents of boarding suggest, 'deprived'. A deprived child is insecure already and his contact with home is normally unreliable. Even so, children whose parents find them difficult often get on better away from the tension of home. The child from a broken home, or whose parents are often on the move, needs the stability of at least one aspect of his life preserved. A boarding school does this.

The upper and upper-middle classes have been sending their sons and daughters to boarding schools for generations. Personal insecurity is not an obvious attribute of these classes: they are in fact conspicuously self-assured.

Children also like routine. It gives them a sense of security. In the same way they like rules, and boarding-school rules are rarely unreasonable. They make it possible for school life to function. The principle of keeping rules becomes a habit in boarding school, and afterwards the child finds it easier to accept standards of adult society.

The boarding-schools' academic reputation is based on the facts of smaller classes and traditions of sixth-form work. Other things being equal, academic standards are likely to be higher in boarding schools. The child's whole environment is an academic one. He can concentrate without distraction. The pattern of daily life allows for sports and recreation, but it also makes time for private work. Day-school 'homework' is no substitute for 'prep'. What is more, the boarding-school child has teachers and libraries constantly at hand. Local public libraries are no substitute; they vary enormously in accessibility and quality, and in any case are not designed specifically for school children. The time that many day pupils spend in dreary and wasteful daily travel is better spent.

The teachers too have a better chance to be good. They are on the spot. They, too, are better able to concentrate on their job. They know their pupils better and can better understand their needs. Boarding-school teachers have other advantages. A parent emotionally involved with his child (what parent is not?) is often the worst person to deal properly with the child's upbringing. A teacher is objective. He is experienced in handling children and their problems. The boarding-school teacher know the child and can inspire his confidence. Most children have a phase when they respect their teachers more than their parents, and here the boarding-school teacher can be of more positive use than his day-school colleague.

It is not only academic facilities that are better in boarding school. In a boarding school, the child's home for so much of the year, the environmental unit is enormous. All the things he might not have at hand at home – space indoors and out, books, hobbies, friends – are available on the grand scale. The child has without effort a vast range of choice. Normally, there is more room for sports, more time for hobbies. Playing fields are adequate and on the spot: school societies have a recognized place. In short a boarding-school child's time is organized so that he can get the most out of work and play. He is assured that his study time will always be quiet and uninterrupted. He will have all the books he wants and expert help if he needs it. During his leisure time or sports periods his companions will be free to share his pleasures without anyone having to go home for an early tea or to help with the shopping or washing up. The boarding school is a community organized specifically for the children in it. It meets their needs without distraction. It is a microcosm of life in the world outside and children who come to grips with it (as most do) learn how to come to grips with the adult world.

People who complain of the social advantages of boarding schools do not seem to realize that this is an argument in favour of them, not against. If a school will give their child a secure place in the world, why not choose it? It is a fact of national life that boarding schools have intimate connections with Oxford and Cambridge and with business. Why not buy this for your child? A boarding school is at worst a cheap investment – one parent has estimated that it is worth at least £200 a year to a child for the rest of his life. Similarly, opponents of boarding schools complain that the children come from a single social background, but this too is an argument in their favour. Wise parents choose their children's friends. It is sensible for your child to be at a school where his class-mates' parents think as you do. A little bit of snobbery is a small price to pay for these obvious advantages.

It has yet to be proved that the best way of dealing with the problems of adolescents is to throw boys and girls together at the crucial time. All the arguments against co-educational schools apply here with added force. Boys and girls develop at different rates and at different ages. At a boarding school a child can get through the period of adolescence without the distraction and the constant presence of the opposite sex. There is time enough for children to get to know the opposite sex after they leave school, when they are older and wiser. The idea that boarding schools produce homosexuals and lesbians is an obvious myth. Homosexual behaviour is common in all classes through society whether people have been to boarding schools or not.

The chief arguments against boarding school are that the schools are closed, authoritarian and restrictive.

Children thrive better in bad homes than in good institutions. A child's emotional life-line is his relationship with his parents. Boarding school undermines this and offers nothing in its place. The image of loving parents in the background is not enough – especially for young children who are not capable of abstraction. It is not the length of time a child is away from home that makes him feel cut off. Parental authority is usurped by the school: parents themselves have to keep its rules. Children are not free to see their parents when they wish. A boarding-school child does not know his parents. When he comes home at the end of term, his parents are strangers. By the time he has got used to them again at the end of a holiday he has to return to school. Because he sees his parents so infrequently he regards all contact with adults outside school as a privilege rather than a natural right. The whole grown-up world is unnaturally remote. Of course many children survive boarding school. Some do not, and there is no way of telling whether a child will suffer during the years away from home. Having sent him, pressures of money invested and the difficulty of finding another school are against removing him. Even children from 'problem' families need not get on better in boarding schools. The more difficult a child is the more he needs individual care and the less likely he is to get it away from home. In fact, homes caring for children separated from their parents have realized the importance of boarding children in small informal family groups. This necessary revolution has not reached the ordinary boarding school.

The closed world of a boarding school is tribal and authoritarian. It trains children into accepting hierarchies. Progress through the school is seen to bring increasing privileges including trivial ones like wearing clothes a certain way or walking on a particular piece of grass. Unlovable aspects of ordinary schools are emphasized at boarding schools. These include undue submission to authority, unquestioning parochial loyalty, the subordination, often menial, of younger children to older ones, and various forms of snobbery. They produce on the one hand people who are over-submissive to those above, dependent on hierarchy and arrogant to those below, and on the other hand people with a disregard for all rules and conventions. The regimentation of boarding school only makes children aware of their lack of freedom. It delays the time when they must learn to organize their own lives and it means that they can develop their private interests (if these conflict with group interests) only by rebellion.

A child's study should take place among, and as one of, the ordinary activities of life. School is not like adult society and learning to live in school is not preparing for life outside. The problems and difficulties of democracy are not made easier by education in a tight authoritarian community. The idea that children in boarding schools meet others of different ages is a myth. Such friendships are normally considered taboo, sexual or both. A child may be free to judge his contemporaries without parental pressure but he is subject instead to the pressures of tradition and mass opinion, which are worse.

Punishment in boarding school tends to be regressive. Beating and drills are common in boys' schools. Physical exhaustion is frequently used as a punishment. Punishment is often administered by the older pupils, which is bad for both punisher and punished. The prefect system is at best silly: if the prefects beat, it is nasty as well.

If boarding schools have high academic standards it is because they have such favourable pupil-teacher ratios. It is this, not the fact of boarding, that is important. Indeed there is evidence that, allowing for intelligence and social class, boarding schools do less well academically than day schools. Making a child responsible for his own homework rather than setting compulsory periods of prep encourages responsibility. No school library is as good as a good public library to which a day-school child will have access. An awful lot of time in boarding school is wasted in compulsory and irrelevant pursuits. Moreover, if a child is unhappy no amount of good teaching or facilities will make him achieve academic success. Even if he does well academically, this is not sufficient reason for bringing him up as a cloistered individual, knowing little about the ordinary business of living. No teacher can give a child the special care he naturally gets at home. Relationships between children and teachers are formal. A child can seldom confide in a teacher. Staff changes aggravate this and upset any attachment a child may have for a teacher as a parent-figure.

Not all teachers are good. A bad boarding-school teacher is more dangerous than a bad day-school teacher. A child's dislike for a particular teacher affects both his achievements in school subjects and his emotional stability. In any case, are teachers the best people to handle children? There is something odd about anyone who shuts himself off in a single-sex institution. A glance at some boarding-school rules suggests doubts about the wisdom of the people who enforce them.

There are many day schools which have room for sports and school societies, and these are normally more free from pressure to take part in them. No school can provide what most communities offer. A day-school child has a choice of theatres, concerts and cinemas. He is not limited to the few outings which the school may arrange. More important, he knows that his needs and pleasures are not the only things to be considered. He learns to fit in with society at large. He can meet people of different abilities and backgrounds in political, church and youth club activities.

Social distinctions are becoming less and less relevant, even in Britain. It is less and less likely that children will be able to get on through influence. It is far better for children and far more 'character-building' if they get where they want to be through their own work rather than through influence. The fact that other children have parents with similar incomes to your own is no guarantee of their desirability. Children need to learn that there are people in all social groups who can be good friends to them. They will get more out of life and be much nicer people if they know this.

Keeping the sexes apart in adolescence does not eliminate sex. It merely turns it in homosexual directions. The idea that children in boarding schools are not troubled by sex is nonsense. Single-sex boarding schools are simply unnatural. Compromises like the sixth-form dance ('no lipstick' – 'keep the lights on, please') are no basis for normal contact between boys and girls. Both boys and girls are sent to boarding schools at exactly the wrong time. Boys normally go at 8, which is too young. They are developmentally behind girls and suffer more from school worries. Girls usually start at 13, in the throes of puberty, when they need the sympathy and reassurance of their mothers. The socially accepted traits of the boarding school child are of the cold and reserved 'typical' Englishman. These are symptoms of disturbance. The children have difficulty in making wholehearted relationships. Parents and substitutes have failed them. The opposite sex has been denied them. To them all human relationships are suspect. Their excessive loyalties to institutions persist as infantile substitutes throughout life. What else is the old school tie?

NURSERY SCHOOLS

The argument for nursery schools is that children enjoy them because they offer somewhere to play and meet other children in a safe place specifically designed for them. Children become sociable at a very early age and want to be with other children. If children are not given the chance to be sociable at an age when they first want it, they can remain shy and withdrawn for the rest of their lives. They also enjoy a change of scenery. The nursery schools offer all this together with trained staff and proper equipment. They are doubly necessary in towns where children might otherwise have no room to play in safety or meet others. Nor should the interests of mothers be overlooked. They have a much better chance of being good if the sheer burden of their children is not incessant. Another advantage of the nursery school is that it smoothes the transition into full-time primary school at 5. (See also pages 80–83.)

The chief argument against nursery schools is that children are too young to leave home and that under the age of 5 their place is with their mothers. Many 5-year-olds are bewildered and exhausted by school and to send them earlier is unnatural and cruel. However freely a nursery school is organized, the children will have to be regimented to some extent. They are at an age when they need the full-time love and care of their mothers and when good mothers want the children at home with them. The children will be away at school soon enough at 5, and children in all other countries go to school later – at 6 or even 7. Nothing can compensate for the basic security of the family.

STAYING ON AT SCHOOL

Most educated people assume that children ought to stay on at school for as long as possible – and even longer at university and college. This view is not universal, however, and the fact that children are reaching puberty earlier is raising more doubts. The present school-leaving age is 15: it will be 16 in 1972–3.

The argument for staying on is that children develop so much in adolescence and are only then able to learn the really important things of life. To leave school at 15 is to enter adult life with an education appropriate only to a child. Adolescence is quite difficult enough without its taking place in a new and alien environment. A school is designed for the children in it: the adult world is not. The benefits of staying on at school are reflected also in the individual's increased earning power. It is true that some schools are not very good and give their pupils a sense of waste and futility – but this is an argument for improving the schools, not for turning out children into something worse, like a factory.

An argument against staying on is that although schools may be designed for children, they are not designed for adolescents. A boy or girl wants to take on new adult responsibilities and should be encouraged to do so. Going to work and earning money may give them a new sense of purpose, and there are many jobs where further education and training is possible. It is not good for young people to be a drain on their parents and the community for longer than is necessary.

STREAMING

Probably most teachers are in favour of streaming. The chief arguments in its favour are that it is the most effective way of dividing very large groups, that children work best when they are with others of similar ability, that teachers themselves have a better chance to be good with a more homogeneous group, and that it is possible for a syllabus, textbooks and standards to be quite delicately matched to a rapid or a slow pace of learning. Children who show sudden improvement or deterioration can be moved from one stream to another.

There is quite a lot of criticism of streaming from parents, particularly in the junior school. The complaint is that with the best will in the world (which is often lacking) streaming is too rigid, and a child selected for the A stream at 7 is already pre-selected for the 11+: a child put in the B stream at the earlier age is, so to speak, pre-rejected. There is less criticism of streaming at the secondary stage, though teachers in secondary modern schools are often articulate about its dire effects, on morale, progress, and behaviour, in the C and D streams. There is also some feeling that the D streams of grammar schools represent a kind of sunken problem. The other arguments against streaming are normally put in social rather than educational terms. Children should not be segregated from other, different children for their school lives, and streaming is said to reflect social rather than educational differences anyway (more middle-class children are in the top streams). It is bad for the lower streams and it encourages teachers to treat children as classes, not as individuals. Some brave opponents of streaming say that the bright children learn more by helping others.

FAMILY GROUPING

Family grouping, or vertical classification, has been introduced recently into a few infant schools. In this form of organization the age-range of each class is extended from one to two or three years. All the classes in an infant school might contain children between five and seven years old, and an individual child would remain in the same class throughout his infant school life, instead of 'going up' from class one to class two and then class three.

The basic argument for it is that it extends the range of attainment that teachers might expect from their pupils and makes it easier for them to provide for children who are exceptionally able or retarded. The newcomers to each class are a relatively small group and come into a settled community which might contain older siblings or neighbours' children (hence 'family grouping'). The new entrants learn by imitating older children. Older ones who are slightly backward, for instance in reading, can still use the simpler books. The teachers can concentrate more easily on individuals and small groups at their particular stage of development.

The chief argument against it is that it demands too much of teachers. It is not only that they need great skill in dealing with diverse groups: if a child spends the whole of his infant school life with one teacher that teacher must be good. There is the obvious possibility that the younger children will be overshadowed and the older ones under-extended.

CHAPTER NINE

Further and Higher Education

ANY account of further and higher education that is coherent is almost bound to be misleading. The range of institutions and levels and types of work is enormous, and there are no tidy dividing lines between one sort of institution and another. This chapter is offered as a guide through the confusion.

It may be as well to start with definitions. Further education is the third of the stages of education mentioned in the 1944 Act. It is defined in the Act (Section 41) as 'full time and part time education for persons over compulsory school age; and leisure-time occupation, in such organized cultural training and recreative activities as are suited to their requirements, for any persons over compulsory school age who are able and willing to profit by the facilities provided for that purpose'. (Secondary education, it will be remembered, includes provision for senior pupils up to 19 years of age. So the definition of further education must be qualified so as to exclude education in secondary schools. In other words, an 18-year-old taking A level at a grammar school is still in the secondary stage and not in further education.)

Higher education is not defined in the 1944 Act. Before 1944 it meant something quite different from what it means now. The Committee on Higher Education (the Robbins Committee) which reported in 1963 was asked 'to review the pattern of full-time higher education' and covered part-time higher education only in passing. Perhaps the most useful definition would be something like this: higher education is full-time or part-time education leading to qualifications more advanced than G.C.E. A level or Ordinary National Certificate. This definition (unlike many others) includes courses which a student can begin without A level but whose final examination is beyond it, for example teacher training and some professional qualifications.

I) THE PUBLIC SECTOR

The definition of further education in the Act is, of course, very wide indeed, but it is doubtful if anyone in 1944 foresaw the subsequent growth and development of the technical colleges. By 1963, ten of them had so developed that the Robbins Committee said they should become universities, and they did so in 1966 or 1967. Now dozens of them have been designated, singly or in groups, as 'polytechnics' or comprehensive institutions of higher education. Indeed it has been Government policy since 1965 to recognize a 'binary' system of higher education, one sector of which is represented by the universities and the other by the local authority technical, commerce, and art colleges and colleges of education.

Technical Colleges

Perhaps the most astonishing development of all those which flowed from the Education Act, 1944, has been this growth and evolution of the technical colleges. Technical education started in Britain in the middle of the 19th century, and its real heyday was in the 1880s and 1890s when a technical college was founded in most major cities. After that the colleges went through half a century of national neglect. Since 1945 they have grown rapidly and greatly extended their range of work, to include, for example, G.C.E. O and A level and degrees. They have retained, however, their distinctive traditions, which contrast with those of the universities. These can be summarized as follows. The colleges are concerned with professional and vocational education (as distinct from 'knowledge for its own sake'); they have no formal entry requirements, and a student can take a course at the level appropriate to him; they have close links with industry and commerce; they put on any course for which there is a demand; they accommodate part time and evening students; they are primarily teaching rather than research institutions. In 1956 the colleges were 'rationalized', and this still forms the basis of their distribution over the country.

Most of the colleges, nearly 300 in number and going under the name of technical college, college of technology, municipal college, technical institute, or college of further education, are mainly concerned with work of the level of Ordinary National Certificates and below, including City and Guilds courses, G.C.E. O and A level and Royal Society of Arts examinations. They offer chiefly part time courses and much of their work is done in the evenings. But they do have some full time courses and may offer some advanced work.

There are another 160 colleges offering much the same range of courses as those above but having also more advanced work, going up to the level of the Higher National Certificate and, in some colleges, degrees. Most of their students are studying part time and below advanced level, but of the full time advanced students nearly half are studying arts and social sciences. The colleges also offer courses in art and commerce.

Perhaps we ought to include here the two dozen colleges of commerce, some of which are developing full time work.

Regional Colleges

In the twenty regional colleges something like half the students are doing advanced work, in courses leading to higher national certificates and diplomas, professional qualifications and degrees, though over half of them are working part time and in the evenings. Just over a third of all the students are studying full time. Some of the colleges have courses for higher degrees and some research. It is in these colleges that the range, type, and level of work is greatest: they are in this sense 'comprehensive' institutions.

National Colleges

There used to be six national colleges established and financed jointly by the Department of Education and Science and particular industries to offer advanced technical studies in those industries. They covered food technology; rubber technology; heating, ventilating, refrigeration and fan engineering; and foundry technology. Most of them have recently been incorporated in other institutions leaving only two, the National College of Agricultural Engineering in Bedfordshire and the National Leathersellers' College in London as independent institutions. The College of Aeronautics at Cranfield provides advanced technological education at postgraduate level only.

Other Establishments

In addition to all this there are 135 art establishments, 4 agricultural colleges and 41 farm institutes.

C.A.T.s

In 1956 eight technical colleges were designated as colleges of advanced technology (C.A.T.s), and another two were designated later. They were meant to be the apex of the technical college pyramid and were to concentrate on full time work of degree level and above. In particular they were to prepare students for the Diploma in Technology (see page 179). The ten colleges became direct grant institutions in 1962 and, following the recommendations of the Robbins Committee, they became university institutions during 1966 and 1967 (see pages 189, 193).

Polytechnics

In 1966 a White Paper was published called *A Plan for Polytechnics and Other Colleges*, and subtitled 'higher education in the further education system'. The attempt was again made to concentrate full time courses of higher education (that is, university level) in a substantially smaller number of centres. It was announced that the Secretary of State would designate about thirty 'polytechnics' which would be either single technical colleges, or groups of these, or groups of technical, art, and commerce colleges. (Two polytechnics include colleges of education and five have education departments.) There were to be no more designations for ten years. The polytechnics were to be 'comprehensive academic communities . . . for students at all levels of higher education'. So far 28 polytechnics have been designated, two others based on colleges at Enfield, Hendon and Hornsey, in North London, and on colleges in Blackburn, North Lancashire will bring the total number to thirty.

Qualifications in Technical Colleges

The qualifications available to students in the various colleges are extraordinarily diverse, and it is only in recent years (since the White Paper of 1961) that they have begun to be rationalized. Even now progress is patchy, and the following account may be somewhat idealized.

Operatives, Apprentices and Technicians

Courses for operatives (who are workers who need some skill but may not be apprentices) are available in chemicals and iron and steel and in the newer processing industries. They are becoming more numerous under the influence of the Industrial Training Act, 1964 (see pages 180–82).

Courses for apprentices are of very long standing. Apprenticeship implies a bargain: the apprentice is paid a wage, he undertakes to learn, and his employer undertakes to teach him. Craft apprentices are indentured normally for five years and are then accepted as fully fledged members of a craft union. Indeed 'craftsman' can mean nothing more than that a man is a member of a craft union: it tells us nothing of the amount of craft he may have learned. Apprenticeship arrangements vary from firm to firm and from one part of the country to another. Attendance at technical college is even now by no means essential to it. Many firms are still reluctant to give apprentices day-release for their studies, though the Industrial Training Act is putting pressure on them.

The colleges offer part time courses for apprentices, leading to the examinations either of the City and Guilds of London Institute or the Royal Society of Arts. For most crafts there are two City and Guilds certificates: 'craft' and 'advanced craft'. Both are taken after part time study, the first for two years and the second for a further two years. The average apprentice goes for the former and the brighter for the latter.

There are new courses, too, for ordinary technicians – other than those who go on to Ordinary National Certificate (see below). They are all run by the City and Guilds and exist, for example, for electrical technicians, mechanical engineering technicians in mining, construction, and shipbuilding. A boy leaving school at 15 may start on a two-year diagnostic course, transfer to a technician course after one year (or to the second year of that course after two) or try for an O.N.C. course after two years. A boy leaving school at 16 might start directly on the technican course.

National Certificates and Diplomas

An attempt is now being made to link the craft and technician courses (at least for promising students) to the national certificate courses. These were started, on the initiative of the Board of Education, in the early 1920s. The certificates and diplomas are awarded by joint committees of the Department of Education and Science and the professional association concerned: for example, the Institution of Mechanical Engineers for the Certificate in Mechanical Engineering. The colleges themselves draw up the syllabuses and set and mark the examination papers. The joint committees approve the syllabuses and appoint assessors for the examinations. The student's work throughout the course counts towards his final result. The certificates are awarded after part time study, the diplomas after full time. The national certificate system has given the colleges a good deal of freedom and flexibility in meeting local needs. At the higher level the awards are comparable with a university pass degree, and the colleges had the freedom to evolve their own courses at a time when new university colleges remained under the tutelage of the University of London.

For the Ordinary National Certificate, the entry qualification is four passes at G.C.E. O level. The main mode of entry is actually getting the four O levels, but there are two others. The first is a general engineering course, taken for two years by boys leaving school at 15 and for one year by boys leaving at 16. The course is diagnostic: those who do well go on to O.N.C. The other method of entry is from the third year of a craft apprenticeship course.

Students who do well in the Ordinary National Certificate have further possibilities open to them. They can go on to the Higher National Certificate or Diploma and then, with further study, to membership of a professional institution, though this route is now being closed. Or they can go on to a degree of the Council for National Academic Awards or of a university.

One can take O.N.C. and O.N.D. in ten subjects each and H.N.C. and H.N.D. in twenty-one subjects each. Building, mining and textile technology can all be taken at both levels and for certificates and diplomas. Civil, electrical and mechanical engineering can be taken only at the higher level; catering and institutional management only in full time courses – and so on.

C.N.A.A. and other Degrees

The Council for National Academic Awards was set up in 1964, on the recommendation of the Robbins Committee. The Council grants degrees to students successfully completing courses of higher education in 'non-autonomous' institutions – like the technical colleges. The Council's predecessor was the National Council for Technological Awards which since 1955 had awarded the Diploma in Technology and Membership of the College of Technologists to students successfully completing courses which it had approved at colleges of advanced technology and other technical colleges. It had granted the diploma, rather than a degree, in deference to university diehardism – though the diploma was recognized by universities, Government and industry as comparable with an honours degree. The distinctive feature of courses leading to the diploma was the 'sandwich' principle – an integrated course in which practical training and experience in industry were combined with academic work, either in alternate six months or in a single year in the middle of the course. This principle remains important in C.N.A.A. degrees. As before, the Council approves courses which may lead to its degrees: the colleges themselves prepare the courses and set and mark the examinations. There are, of course, external examiners to secure a reasonable equivalence of standards, just as there are in most universities.

As its name implied, the old Diploma in Technology covered a limited range of studies, mainly in engineering and other technologies. The degrees of the new council can be awarded in any subject. Technologies still predominate, but business studies and the social sciences are expanding fast.

In addition to the C.N.A.A. degrees, a number of technical colleges still prepare students for the external degree of the University of London. In 1969 2,000 students gained C.N.A.A. degrees and nearly 3,000 gained external London degrees from technical and other colleges.

The Industrial Training Act, 1964

The work of the technical and other colleges is being increasingly influenced by the Industrial Training Act, 1964, which is not an Education Act at all. The Act has three main objects: to get enough properly trained people at all levels of industry; to improve the quality of industrial training; and to share its cost more evenly among firms. It gave the Minister of Labour the power to set up industrial training boards and a Central Training Council. Education members are in a very small minority on both the council and the boards – most members are employers or trade unionists – but the Department of Education and Science does provide an assessor for each board.

There will soon be about thirty industrial training boards covering most of industry and commerce. Their duties are: to recommend the nature, content and length of training (including associated further education) appropriate for occupations in their industries; and to ensure adequate facilities for it. Boards also have powers to cooperate with the Youth Employment Service, to arrange for tests of attainment and selection tests, and to engage in or assist research.

Each board imposes a levy on employers and can pay grants to those who do training, or arrange for it, which meets the board's requirements. A firm which offers no training pays a levy but gets no grant: a firm which does more than its share of good training gets more back in grant that it pays in levy. Subject to approval by the Minister of Labour, each board determines the rate of levy for its industry, and its education members do not vote on the levy. Each board also receives grants from the Ministry of Labour towards the cost of certain items of training and for its administrative costs for the first year.

To take an example, the engineering board, which began operating in 1965–6, imposes a '2½ per cent on pay roll' levy, which raised £75m. in its first year. The board distributes most of this income as a general grant to employers based on an assessment of their training arrangements. Specific grants are made for certain kinds of training which the board particularly wishes to encourage. For example, the specific grant for first year off-the-job training of craftsmen and technicians fully satisfying the board's requirements is £504 per trainee for schemes lasting 48 weeks, or 10 guineas a week per trainee for shorter schemes at least 24 weeks long. A grant of £50 is paid for schemes which do not satisfy the board's requirements but which offer paid day or block release throughout the technical college session.

An important principle behind the Act is that a board's recommendation on training for a particular job should cover the associated further education. The Central Training Council has said that the purpose of this further education is : to provide a knowledge and appreciation of techniques to enable a trainee to do his job; to inculcate a broad understanding of science and technology so that the trainee understands associated occupations and can adjust to changes in his work; to widen his understanding of society and develop him as a person; and to prepare suitable trainees for advanced study leading to more highly skilled work.

So far, existing further education courses have usually been associated with proposed training but there have been important exceptions to this. For example, the engineering board's first-year proposals gave rise to a completely new one year part time course of further education – the Basic Engineering Craft Certificate course – which was devised by the City and Guilds of London Institute and the Regional Examining Unions, and introduced in some colleges in the academic year 1966–7.

When industrial training, as distinct from further education, is provided in technical colleges, it is frequently in the form of one year full time courses of combined education and training. In engineering alone, the places on these integrated courses increased from 1,400 in 1965–6 to 8,500 in 1966–7 after the publication of the engineering board's recommendations for first year off-the-job training. The cost of the industrial training element in these integrated courses is met by employers, who claim appropriate grant from their boards. To avoid complicated calculations over fees, 60 per cent of all integrated courses are deemed to consist of training, the remainder of further education, and charges are made on a uniform national basis.

The Industrial Training Act is a reactionary piece of legislation. The contrast with the Robbins Report, published at the same time as the original Bill, was stark. For a minority there was to be higher education 'to promote the general powers of the mind' – for the great majority industrial training primarily for the benefit of employers. There is a conflict inherent in all vocational education. The employer sees it as a way of getting better workmen: the employee as a way of getting a better job (and the Robbins Report applauded this latter aim for higher education). The Industrial Training Act tips the balance in favour of the employer in an almost Victorian way. At the same time it reduces the academic freedom of the colleges. It is one thing to react to social and industrial demand; it is another to have one's syllabuses imposed from outside. The Act is a very good example of a change made for a limited purpose (to spread the costs of training) having very much larger consequences in areas it was not equipped to tackle.

Its final, and perhaps unintended, consequence was to kill the idea of county colleges (see below). These were misconceived too, in that they were based on the assumption that most people's jobs would be so awful that all one could do was to improve their leisure. But they have been a dead letter, not because it was thought out and decided that they should be, but through sheer inadvertence.

County Colleges

County colleges were one of the most important ways in which further education was to be provided under the 1944 Act. Local authorities were required to establish them as centres for further education, including physical, practical and vocational training, for people between the compulsory school-leaving age and 18 who were not in full time education. This education was to enable them to develop their various aptitudes and capacities and to prepare them for the responsibilities of citizenship. The young persons were to attend the county colleges for one whole day or two half days a week, for forty-four weeks a year. Alternatively, where suitable, the young person was to be compelled to attend continuously either for eight weeks or for two periods of four weeks each a year. There were similar regulations for enforcing attendance as exist for enforcing attendance at school. So far no county colleges as such have been built, and this part of the Act is a dead letter.

Adult Education

Another way in which further education was to be offered under the Act was in what is largely called 'adult education', at evening institutes or in cooperation with voluntary bodies like the Workers' Educational Association. The variety of these is very great. People may wish to patch the rather ragged education they got at school. They may attend, for example, two nights a week to learn a foreign language. They may go for more broadly cultural classes – in literature, musical appreciation, or local history. They may pursue a hobby, like drama, pottery or cooking, or seek to gain some grasp of the world around them through classes in economics, politics or current affairs. These classes may be run by the Workers' Educational Association, by the universities, or by the local authorities.

The courses run by local authorities are likely to be in evening institutes: the classes take place in the evening in schools or colleges that are used during the day for the normal education of children. During the academic year 1969–70 over a million people attended evening institutes, two-thirds of them women. The largest single age-group was the one which had just left school, but two-thirds of the total consisted of people aged 21 and over. All these attendances were, of course, voluntary.

The Youth Service

The 1944 Act also imposed on the local authorities the duty of providing for the leisure of young people. When it began, over twenty years ago, the youth service was run by voluntary organizations, but in 1947 the Ministry of Education asked the local authorities to integrate it closely with the schools, the youth employment service, and the projected county colleges. Even so, the Albemarle committee reported in 1960 that the service was in a state of acute depression. After that the Ministry of Education announced a building programme and a training programme for youth leaders. The Department of Education and Science gives grants to the national headquarters of various voluntary organizations and towards approved capital expenditure of local youth organizations. The local authorities also give grants towards local capital expenditure and towards maintenance costs, including the salaries of youth leaders. The authorities themselves also provide youth clubs and centres, camps and camp sites, sailing clubs, and so on. They run short conferences, training courses, rallies, and the like. A national college for training youth leaders was opened at Leicester in 1961.

Colleges of Education

The courses at colleges of education are described on pages 68–70. It is probably enough to add here that there are 125 training institutions run by the local authorities, 53 run by voluntary bodies, and 33 by the universities. Of these, 159 are general colleges (107 of which are run by the local authorities) and the rest specialize in particular subjects: 6 in housecraft, 7 in physical education, 13 in art, and 4 in training technical teachers. Two polytechnics include former colleges of education and five have education departments. Of the university institutions 30 are departments of education and 3 are art training centres. By the autumn of 1969 there were over 116,000 students in colleges of education. Since 1960 their courses have been three years long.

All colleges of education, though administered by the local education authorities or voluntary bodies, are linked for academic purposes with universities through institutes of education. The institutes also contain the university departments of education which give one-year courses of teacher training to graduates. They supervise and coordinate the academic work of the colleges of education, approve syllabuses and conduct examinations. They also provide further training for serving teachers and conduct research.

Since the Robbins Report, it has been possible to take a four-year course at a college of education, leading to a B.Ed. (bachelor of education) degree of the university to which the college is linked. A few universities made their first B.Ed. awards in 1968. In 1970 2,268 B.Eds. were awarded. This development represents something of a breakthrough: until now the universities have resolutely refused to acknowledge education as a suitable subject for a degree.

The Open University

The Open University is a curious anomaly: it started life as part of the Labour Party's campaign before the 1964 election, as the University of the Air. The idea was to use television and radio, together with correspondence courses, libraries, study centres and short (perhaps residential) courses, to bring degree level courses to adults who might have missed them when young. It is autonomous like other universities, though getting its funds direct from the Department of Education and Science, not through the University Grants Committee. Degrees are obtained by amassing 'credits' gained in one year courses. Certificates are issued for credits obtained: six credits are needed for an ordinary degree, eight for honours. The B.B.C. provides television and radio broadcasts. The university enrolled its first 24,000 students for courses beginning in January 1971. Its academic year runs from January to December, with examinations in the last two months. Students can get advice from counsellors and tutors at over

250 study centres, equipped with TV and radio. Each student has a course tutor who corrects and returns written work with comment, and attends a one-week summer school for a foundation course. Further information can be obtained from the Admissions Office, The Open University, P.O. Box 48, Bletchley, Bucks.

II) THE UNIVERSITIES

The universities of England and Wales are a very mixed bunch. Like Topsy, they just growed. The only generalization one can make is that students go to them at 18 after gaining two or more subject passes at A level, follow on average a three-year course and emerge with a 'degree'. The degree is granted by the university itself and not by an outside body. For convenience the universities can be grouped under six headings: Oxford and Cambridge, the Scottish universities, London and Wales, the civic universities, the new universities, and the former colleges of advance technology.

Oxford and Cambridge

By far the oldest are Oxford and Cambridge, which started as guilds of teachers who settled in the two towns towards the end of the twelfth century. Foreign-born scholars were expelled from the University of Paris in 1167, and many of them settled in Oxford. There was a migration of scholars from Oxford to Cambridge in 1209. In the thirteenth century benefactors founded residential colleges or halls, first for scholars, then for scholar-teachers and students, and colleges have gone on being founded right up to the present. There are now over two dozen colleges and halls for men, 5 colleges for women and 5 postgraduate colleges at Oxford; there are 21 colleges for men, 4 colleges for women and 3 postgraduate colleges at Cambridge. Most colleges have up to 300 undergraduates, but a few have very many more. It is the colleges which are the outstanding characteristics of Oxford and Cambridge. The university examines, confers degrees, provides the central libraries and laboratories and most of the lectures. Each college, however, is completely independent as far as its property, finance and internal affairs are concerned, and it is by becoming a member of the college that the student becomes a member of the university. For some part of his university life he lives in college and dines regularly in hall. He can always use his college chapel, library and Junior Common Room, and join college clubs and societies; and he is taught, supervised and prepared for final degree examinations by the senior members or fellows of his college. Both Oxford and Cambridge have over 10,000 undergraduate and postgraduate students.

Scottish Universities

Next in age are the ancient Scottish universities. Three of them – St Andrews, Glasgow and Aberdeen – date from the fifteenth century. A fourth, Edinburgh, was established in the sixteenth century. St Andrews and Aberdeen have incorporated other foundations all dating from the fifteenth and sixteenth centuries, but the collegiate system never caught on as in Oxford and Cambridge. In the last few years Dundee has become independent of St Andrews, the Royal College of Technology, Glasgow, has become the University of Strathclyde, Heriot-Watt College in Edinburgh has become the Heriot-Watt University, a new University of Stirling has just been opened. Edinburgh has over 9,000 students, Glasgow over 7,000, and Strathclyde over 5,000; Aberdeen has over 5,000; Dundee and St Andrews over 2,000; Heriot-Watt has nearly 2,500 and Stirling 600.

London and Wales

London and Wales are both federal universities. The University of London is the largest in the country: with over 31,500 students, it has half as many as all the civic universities put together. It was established in the early nineteenth century as a protest against the denominational tests then imposed for entry into Oxford and Cambridge. From the middle of that century its degrees have been available for students other than those in recognized institutions, and these 'external' degrees still make possible an academic award of high standing for students at home and abroad who are not at the university. London was also the first university in the kingdom to admit women to its degrees (in 1888). Four of London's colleges – Bedford, King's, Queen Mary and University Colleges – and three specialist schools – Imperial College of Science and Technology, the London School of Economics, and Chelsea College of Science and Technology – are each as big as some of the civic universities; but these are only seven of the fifteen non-medical colleges or schools of the university. There are thirteen medical schools associated with hospitals, a number of university institutes (of archaeology, of Commonwealth studies, of education and so on), three theological schools and a number of postgraduate medical schools. All these are incorporated in the federation which is the university and which acts as a teaching as well as an examining body.

The University of Wales is also federal, consisting of the four university colleges at Aberystwyth, Cardiff, Bangor and Swansea, the Welsh National School of Medicine, Cardiff, the Institute of Science and Technology, Cardiff, (formerly the Welsh College of Advanced Technology) and St David's, Lampeter. The whole university has nearly 14,000 students.

Civic Universities

The civic universities, which together have nearly 70,000 students, have emerged in their full status only in this century. The main idea behind their foundation was to set up centres of higher education for the areas in which they were established. They were not residential on the Oxford and Cambridge pattern and even now few offer residential accommodation to more than a quarter of their undergraduates, though these come from all over the country. Most of them started as colleges set up by communities or local individual benefactors. The first was Owen's College in Manchester (1851), followed by the Yorkshire College of Science in Leeds (1874), University College, Bristol (1876), colleges at Sheffield, Birmingham, Liverpool, Nottingham Reading, Exeter, and in the twentieth century, Southampton,

Leicester, and Hull. Until they attained full university status these colleges prepared their students for external degrees of the University of London. At one moment it looked as though the colleges would be brought together in federations, but the trend was abruptly halted in 1900, when Birmingham got its own charter as a university. The University of Durham was a theological foundation in 1832 with a collegiate pattern. It used to be a federal university with King's College, Newcastle-upon-Tyne, but Newcastle became independent in 1963.

Many of the colleges achieved full status only after the second world war. There are over 8,000 students at Manchester and over 3,000 in the affiliated Institute of Science and Technology. Leeds has nearly 9,000; Birmingham, Bristol and Liverpool over 6,500; Newcastle and Sheffield over 5,500. Nottingham and Reading have around 5,000; Hull and Southampton have around 4,000 and Durham, Exeter and Leicester over 3,000.

New Universities

The universities founded since the war have been independent from the start, and not under the tutelage of London. They were set up partly because city-centre land round the older universities was thought to be too expensive for expansion, partly because many universities feared to grow and partly because innovation was hoped for. This last expectation has been somewhat fulfilled. The very first of the new universities, Keele, offered nothing but joint honours degrees to combat overspecialization in undergraduates, and many of the others have made similar innovations. Now most of the new universities have over 2,000 students: Sussex (at Brighton) has over 3,500, and Keele 1,800. The others are East Anglia (Norwich), Essex (Colchester), Kent (Canterbury), Lancaster, Warwick and York.

Former Colleges of Advanced Technology

In 1956 ten leading technical colleges were designed as colleges of advanced technology, to concentrate on full-time work at advanced or university level. After a recommendation of the

Robbins Committee they all achieved university status, eight of them becoming independent universities and two becoming colleges of federal universities. Most of the universities now have between 2,000 and 3,000 students. The innovation they have brought into the university world is the sandwich course, in which practical training in industry is integrated with academic work. The universities, with their former names in brackets, are: Aston in Birmingham (the College of Advanced Technology, Birmingham), Bath University of Technology (Bristol College of Science and Technology), Bradford (Bradford Institute of Technology), Brunel (Brunel College, Acton), City (Northampton C.A.T., London), Loughborough University of Technology (Loughborough College of Technology), Salford (Royal College of Advanced Technology) and Surrey (Battersea College of Advanced Technology). Chelsea College of Science and Technology has joined London University and the Welsh C.A.T. has become the University of Wales Institute of Science and Technology.

Independence and Money

All the universities are independent and self-governing. Oxford and Cambridge are governed entirely by members of the university, and each college is a self-governing corporate body. In other universities the governing bodies include lay members elected as representatives of outside bodies. Three-quarters of the income of the universities comes from Exchequer grants, under a tenth from students' fees (three-quarters of which are paid by the local education authorities), more than a tenth from payments for work done by universities, and the rest from endowments, grants from local authorities, donations, and other sources. The money from Exchequer grants (some £200m. in 1968–9) is distributed through the University Grants Committee after consultation with the universities. This means that the universities are not directly responsible to the Secretary of State for Education and Science or to any other Minister, though the Secretary of State does answer general questions about them in Parliament. Until recently the universities had virtually no connection with the old Minister of Education. The U.G.C. distributed grants directly from the Exchequer, and the Chancellor of the Exchequer answered Parliamentary questions about the universities. From 1968 the Comptroller and Auditor General has had access to the books of the universities and the University Grants Committee and the permanent under-secretary of the Department of Education and Science will be answerable for them to the Public Accounts Committee of the House of Commons. The universities regard this as the first attempt at state control – which it is.

University Degrees

Like everything else in higher education the nomenclature of degrees is confusing. In most universities B.A. (Bachelor of Arts) and B.Sc. (Bachelor of Science) degrees are first degrees in arts and science respectively. At Oxford and Cambridge, however, you get a B.A. regardless of whether you study arts or science, and in Scotland the first arts degree is called M.A. (Master of Arts). There is no B.Sc. at Cambridge and at Oxford the B.Sc. is a higher degree. In most universities M.A.s are higher degrees involving further study and another examination. But at Oxford and Cambridge an honours B.A. can get an M.A. simply by paying for it. For the sake of clarity, therefore, it is best to describe the degrees without calling them by particular names. One must distinguish, from the start, between first degrees and higher degrees.

First Degrees To get a first degree you have to put in full-time attendance at a university (unless you are a candidate for a London University external degree or are an evening student at Birkbeck College, London) for at least three years. For some courses the period is longer: in architecture it may be five years and in medicine six. In some courses you may get exemption from the first year by success at G.C.E. A level, but three years is the minimum nevertheless. Normally students do not change universities in mid-course.

There are two kinds of first degree: pass, ordinary or general, and honours or special. A pass degree involves the study of a number of subjects not all of which are pursued for the full three years and in none of which is there a high amount of specialization. Success depends on passing the various subjects separately at the appropriate standard, and if you fail any one subject you can take it again or substitute another. The honours degree concentrates on a single field of study and its related subjects. Normally the field of specialization is mentioned: you get an honours degree in history, physics, and so on. Success depends on performance in a comprehensive final examination which can be taken only once. Degrees awarded are of first, second, third, or fourth class, and normally the second class is divided into two sections – 2:1 and 2:2. If you fail you are given either a pass degree or some credit towards getting one. Just to confuse the issue still further, there are a few universities (particularly the oldest and the newest) which offer joint honours degrees in which you take more than one subject but go into each no less deeply, though perhaps less comprehensively, than in a single honours degree. Normally it is clear from the start of your course whether you are going to do an honours or a pass degree, but in some cases the two courses are very similar in the early years, and in medicine the final examination is a common one in which outstanding candidates may be awarded honours.

Higher Degrees Higher degrees may be divided into three groups: masterships, the doctorate in philosophy, and the senior doctorates. Candidates for a master's degree (at Oxford and Cambridge these are called B.Phil., B.Litt. or something similar, because the M.A. is what you pay for) normally must already have a good first degree. The course normally takes two years and involves writing a thesis or dissertation on a particular topic. Sometimes a written examination is required as well and there is almost always an oral examination. The doctorate in philosophy, so called whatever your subject, also needs a first degree before you start and is given more often after three years' extra work. You have to write a thesis which makes an original contribution to knowledge. The senior doctorates, the names of which alone depend on a particular subject studied, like D.Litt., D.Sc., require at least a master's degree before you start and are awarded on the basis of published contributions to knowledge.

In most universities external examiners from other universities are brought in to help assess work offered for all degrees. At Oxford and Cambridge the examining is done internally by panels of tutors from the various colleges. University diplomas and certificates are rather more simple affairs, may be full time or part time and may take normally one or two years.

III) THE ROBBINS REPORT

In 1963, a committee appointed by the Prime Minister and chaired by Lord Robbins, presented its report on higher education. Along with the report were six appendices full of statistics. Its most influential recommendation was that there should be a substantial expansion in higher education. This recommendation was based upon projections of the demand for places from qualified school-leavers, and its object was to ensure that competition for entry became no keener than it was in 1961. Since then the projections, as the committee expected, have turned out to be too low. Successive governments have contented themselves with expanding universities to meet the committee's figures, but because there are more qualified applicants it is in fact getting harder to enter university. The other sectors of higher education (the colleges of education and the technical colleges) have been expanding much more rapidly than the committee suggested.

The Robbins Report also recommended changes for the teacher training colleges and colleges of advanced technology. The former were to be renamed colleges of education (they have been) and linked administratively to the universities (they have not). A degree (B.Ed.) was suggested to be taken by selected students at the end of a four-year course. The B.Ed. now exists. The translation of the colleges of technology to universities was recommended by the committee and is now complete. Eight of the colleges have become independent universities: two have become colleges of federal universities. The recommendation that five technological institutions should become S.I.S.T.E.R.S. (Special Institutions for Scientific and Technological Education and Research) has not been adopted.

The Council for National Academic Awards was established as a result of a recommendation of the Robbins Committee, though some members of the committee feel its purpose has been perverted. The Committee saw it as a way of awarding degrees to institutions developing towards university status, whereas the C.N.A.A. has in the event been used to award degrees in the second, 'public' sector of a 'binary' system of higher education.

The report also recommended a separate Minister ('of Art and Science') for higher education, but all sectors of education are now the concern of a single Secretary of State.

IV) THE JAMES REPORT

A report on teacher education and training by a committee chaired by Lord James of Rusholme was published when this book was in page proof. It recommended that teacher training should be seen as falling into three 'cycles': the first, personal education; the second, pre-service training and induction; the third, in-service education and training. The third cycle, it said, should have the highest priority.

For the first cycle, the committee recommended a new two-year course leading to a diploma in higher education (Dip.H.E.). The second cycle should also last two years, the first in college and leading to recognition as a 'licensed teacher'; the next in a school and leading to recognition as a 'registered teacher' and the award of a new professional degree of B.A. (Education).

Teacher education should be administered by Regional Councils for Colleges and Departments of Education (R.C.C.D.E.), and the proposed new diplomas and degrees should be awarded by a National Council for Teacher Education and Training (N.C.T.E.T).

APPENDIX ONE

Books and Publications

Probably the best way to keep abreast of what is going on in education is to read periodicals rather than books. There are two educational journals generally available on bookstalls. They are *The Times Educational Supplement* (7p) and *Education* – the official journal of the Association of Education Committees (7½p). Another weekly publication, *New Society* (10p), also covers education fairly fully.

For specific information, go to reference books. The most compendious is the *Education Committees' Year Book*. Universities are covered by the *Commonwealth Universities' Year Book* and the publications of the Universities Central Council on Admissions. Independent schools are listed in *The Public and Preparatory Schools' Year Book*, *The Girls' School Year Book*, and *The Independent Schools' Association Year Book*. Independent schools recognized as efficient are listed in the Department of Education's *List 70*. *The Year Book of Technical Education and Careers in Industry* covers the scientific and technical sides of further and higher education, and the *Handbook of Colleges and Departments of Education* covers teacher training.

The publications of the Department of Education are a quarry of information: there are innumerable lists, reports and pamphlets, most of which are noticed in the national press as they emerge. The Department's *Annual Report* is a good, brisk (though normally rather complacent) guide to what is going on and its statistics are published separately.

In a class by itself is *The New Law of Education* by Taylor and Saunders. The history of education in England and Wales, the present legal framework, and all the relevant regulations, circulars, and memoranda are extremely well edited. The commentary is exceptionally clear and well written.

If you still want more, have a look at George Baron's *A Bibliographical Guide to the English Educational System*, which lists about 600 books under their subject headings and gives a sentence or two of description for each.

APPENDIX TWO

Educational Organizations

Education bristles with organizations: about 500 of them are listed in the back of the *Educational Committees' Year Book*. A few relevant ones may be mentioned here.

Parents' Organizations

Advisory Centre for Education, 32 Trumpington Street, Cambridge, CB21 QY.

Confederation for the Advancement of State Education, 81 Rustlings Road, Sheffield, S11 7AB.

Council for Children's Welfare, 183 Finchley Road, London NW3.

Pre-school Playgroups Association, 87a Borough High Street, London SE1.

National Federation of Parent-Teacher Associations, 5 Elm Terrace, Tividale Hall Estate, Warley, Worcestershire.

National Society for Mentally Handicapped Children, 86 Newman Street, London W1.

Parents' National Educational Union, Murray House, Vandon Street, London SW1.

Teachers' Organizations

Schools

Joint Committee of the Four Secondary Associations, 29 Gordon Square, London WC1 (Association of Headmistresses Incorporated, Incorporated Association of Headmasters, Association of Assistant Mistresses Incorporated, Incorporated Association of Assistant Masters).

National Association of Head Teachers, Avery House, Brunel Place, Crawley, Sussex.

National Association of Schoolmasters, Swan Court, Waterhouse Street, Hemel Hempstead, Hertfordshire.

National Union of Teachers, Hamilton House, Mabledon Place, London WC1.

Union of Women Teachers, 37 Stephyns Chambers, Bank Court, Hemel Hempstead.

APPENDIX TWO

Further and Higher Education

Association of Teachers in Colleges and Departments of Education, 3 Crawford Place, London, W1H 2BN.

Association of Teachers in Technical Institutions, Hamilton House, Mabledon Place, London wc1.

Association of University Teachers, Bremar House, Sale Place, London w2.

Authorities' Organizations

Association of Education Committees, 10 Queen Anne Street, London w1.

Association of Municipal Corporations, 36 Old Queen Street, London sw1.

County Councils Association, 66a Eaton Square, London sw1.

National Association of Divisional Executives for Education, Education Offices, Walpole Road, Gosport, Hampshire.

National Association of Governors and Managers, 34 Sandilands, Croydon, CRO 5DB.

Welsh Joint Education Committee, 30 Cathedral Road, Cardiff.

APPENDIX THREE

Officials of an Education Authority

A typical large English education authority has the following senior officials:

A chief education officer; a deputy chief education officer; three assistant education officers; a chief county inspector, five county inspectors for schools and one for further education; organizers for art, domestic science, drama, handicrafts, music, physical education (senior organizer), science (2) and visual and aural aids and closed circuit television; a county catering and schools meals officer; a county librarian; a county youth officer; a county careers officer; a principal school medical officer*; a psychologist to the education committee; a county architect*; a county treasurer* and a county supplies officer*. The officials marked * are shared with the other departments of the authority.

This particular authority has an education committee of 39 elected members of the council, 7 representatives of divisional executives and 16 other people selected for their special knowledge, five of whom represent the teachers. They meet six times a year, on Mondays.

The population of the county is over a million and the product of a penny rate is over £225,000. There are 2 nursery schools, 519 primary schools, 111 secondary schools, 4 technical colleges and 3 colleges of further education, 2 colleges of education, 3 residential youth centres, 2 schools of art and 1 residential college for adults. There are also 13 day and 8 residential special schools, and one hospital special school.

APPENDIX FOUR

What a Local Authority Spends

Every year each local education authority has to estimate its coming annual expenditure. It does this on a form – Form 501F – which it sends to the Department of Education and Science. The headings of the form and the totals for a typical authority are given here as an illustration. Each of the totals is analysed, in the complete return, over the following subdivisions: administration and inspection, nursery education, primary education, secondary education, special education, further (including agricultural) education, training of teachers, education research, school health service, facilities for recreation and social and physical training, other education services. It is interesting that over half the total expenditure is for salaries. The heading of the form is self-explanatory: the very last total, 'net expenditure', is the one used to calculate the amount of rate support grant from the Ministry of Housing and Local Government. The appendix to Form 501F covers school meals and milk, which also attract rate support grant.

APPENDIX FOUR

DEPARTMENT OF EDUCATION AND SCIENCE

Education Services Relevant for Rate Support Grant Return of Estimated Net Expenditure

Form 501F 1967/68 L.E.A.———

EXPENDITURE	£
I Employees	
1. Salaries and Wages (including Superannuation & National Insurance)	
(a) Teaching staff	9,970,930
(b) Non-teaching staff	1,828,180
2. All other employees' expenses	3,165
SUB-TOTAL: HEAD I	11,802,275
II Premises	1,924,310
III Supplies and services	1,058,365
IV Establishment expenses	470,795
TOTAL: HEADS I–IV	15,255,745
V Agency Services	
1. Rendered by other local education authorities	
(a) Contributions in respect of individual pupils	1,267,040
(b) Contributions in respect of other services (e.g. jointly mtd. instns.)	—
2. All other agency services (including payments under Section 6 of the Education (Misc. Provisions) Act, 1953	316,215
SUB-TOTAL: HEAD V	1,583,255

WHAT A LOCAL AUTHORITY SPENDS

VI Miscellaneous expenses (including Transport and Heavy Plant and Taxation, but excluding Assistance to Students and Pupils shown in Head VII)
1. Grants to universities and colleges 22,250
2. All other miscellaneous expenses 198,240

SUB-TOTAL: HEAD VI   220,490

TOTAL: HEADS I–VI   17,059,490

VII Assistance to students and pupils
1. Awards and grants
   (a) University awards 730,000
   (b) Other higher or further education awards
       (i) for degree and comparable courses ... 317,000
       (ii) for other courses (including training of teachers)... 661,000
   (c) Salaries etc. of teachers seconded for approved further training 53,140
   (d) Fees and expenses at independent and direct grant schools (Section 81, Education Act, 1944) 129,515
   (e) Maintenance allowances for school pupils over compulsory school age 16,900
   (f) Other awards and grants 34,520
2. Other assistance to students and pupils
   (a) Provision of board and lodging, clothing and footwear 8,865
   (b) Provision of transport between home and school 422,250

SUB-TOTAL: HEAD VII   2,373,190

VIII Debt charges 2,491,550
IX Revenue contributions to capital outlay 335,000
X Appropriations (otherwise than by annual instalments) ... ... —

TOTAL EXPENDITURE: HEADS I–X   22,259,230

APPENDIX FOUR

	INCOME	£
XI	Fees (including tuition and boarding in maintained institutions and examinations)	215,845
XII	1. Contributions to board and lodging of pupils other than in maintained schools, and towards clothing and footwear	15,580
	2. Contributions towards transport between home and school	—
XIII	Contributions by other local education authorities	
	1. In respect of individual pupils	295,365
	2. In respect of other services (e.g. jointly maintained institutions)	—
XIV	Income not included elsewhere	115,060
XV	Appropriations (otherwise than by annual instalments)	—
	TOTAL INCOME: HEADS XI TO XV	641,850
	NET EXPENDITURE	21,617,380

WHAT A LOCAL AUTHORITY SPENDS

Form 501F (Appendix) L.E.A.—————

		ESTIMATE
	PART A – EXPENDITURE	1967–8
I	*School Meals Service*	£
	Dinners at maintained schools	
1.	(i) Gross running expenditure on food	1,017,935
	(ii) Gross running expenditure on overhead costs:	
2.	(a) Salaries and wages including superannuation and National Insurance	1,117,985
3.	(b) Other running expenditure including central administration	362,555
4.	(c) Sub-total	1,480,540
5.	(iii) Total gross running expenditure	2,498,475
6.	(iv) Income	992,085
7.	(v) Net running expenditure	1,506,390
	Non-maintained schools	
8.	Net running expenditure on dinners at non-maintained schools	4,000
9.	*Capital expenditure from revenue*	165,000
10.	*Loan charges*	124,250
11.	SUB-TOTAL	289,250
II	*Milk in Schools Scheme*	
12.	(i) Purchase of Milk	274,775
13.	(ii) Overhead costs	6,220
14.	SUB-TOTAL	280,995
	GRAND TOTAL NEW EXPENDITURE	2,080,635

APPENDIX FOUR

PART B – STATISTICS

(a) Estimated number of dinners to be served in schools maintained by the Authority 21,753,500
(b) Estimated number of feeding days in the year... 196
(c) Cost per meal:
  (i) Food ... ... 11.23d.
  (ii) Overheads ... ... 16.33d.

Glossary of Educational Terms

Parents often feel at a disadvantage when talking about education, because education, like any other subject, has its own specialized vocabulary and jargon. This guide does not claim to be complete but it does contain most of the expressions which educationists are constantly using and which are often puzzling to the ordinary parent. Precise and accurate definitions of the expressions would be longer, more complicated and much less comprehensible than anything in this guide. Many of them occur in the course of this book. The object of the guide is to help to explain rather than to define.

adult education: Spare time study for adults (usually by evening classes) run by local education authorities, universities, and voluntary bodies like the Workers' Educational Association (W.E.A.).

advanced courses: Courses in further (q.v.) and higher (q.v.) education leading to a standard above G.C.E. A level (q.v.) or O.N.C. (q.v.).

agreed syllabus: Syllabus (q.v.) of religious instruction (q.v.) agreed between representatives of a local education authority, religious denominations, and teachers.

aided school: Voluntary school (q.v.) whose governors or managers are responsible for the provision and maintenance of the premises, can appoint and dismiss staff and decide the religious teaching. Almost all aided schools are C. of E. or R.C.

all-age school: School which takes children from 5 to 15. Many village schools were of this type: they have almost disappeared.

ancillary: a paid helper, not a qualified teacher, who assists in a school, e.g. at meal-times.

apprenticeship: Organized scheme of training at work for a specific number of years, leading to acceptance into a recognized trade.

arts subjects: School or university subjects, like languages and history, which are not scientific: not to be confused with the arts, like music and painting.

assistant master (*mistress, teacher*)*:* Anyone on the teaching staff of a school who is not the head teacher.

autonomous institutions: See binary policy.

auxiliary: See ancillary.

award: See scholarship.

GLOSSARY

backwardness: General term to describe the condition of those children who are noticeably less developed than their contemporaries.

bilateral school: Secondary school (q.v.) which is in effect a combination of two schools (e.g. grammar/technical or technical/modern).

binary policy: Term used to describe the fact that higher education is available both in autonomous universities and in the 'public' sector of technical and other colleges and colleges of education.

bipartite system: Description of secondary education as divided between secondary modern and grammar schools (c.f. tripartite system).

boarding school: School whose pupils live on the premises either for whole terms or for shorter periods like a week.

building programme: List of projects approved by the Department of Education and Science to start in a particular financial year.

'bulge', the: Jargon for the increased number of pupils passing through the schools on account of the sharp rise in the birth-rate. One occurred after the war, another in the late fifties.

Burnham committee: Committee, consisting of representatives of the Secretary of State, the teachers and the local education authorities, which agrees teachers' salaries.

bursary: Award similar to a scholarship (q.v.).

capitation allowance: Annual allowance made to a school by a local education authority in respect of each pupil for books, equipment, materials, etc.

Central Advisory Councils: Two bodies (one for England, one for Wales) set up by law to advise the Minister of Education on educational theory and practice. In abeyance since 1967.

Certificate of Secondary Education (C.S.E.): Subject examination (q.v.) taken at the end of secondary education, which may be set and marked by an individual school with external assessment.

chief education officer: Chief permanent, paid official of a local education authority. May also be known as director of education, secretary for education, or simply education officer.

child guidance clinic: Centre run by the local education or other authority to treat maladjustment (q.v.) in children.

child psychiatrist: see psychiatrist.

City and Guilds of London Institute: Largest of the independent examining bodies in technical education.

civic university: University founded in large town originally as a centre of higher education for the area.

class: (1) Group of pupils in a school taking lessons together (see also

GLOSSARY

form, set, stream, year). (2) Rank gained in an honours degree (q.v.).

classics, the: (1) Latin and Greek. (2) Literary works in any language, or musical compositions, permanently judged outstanding.

closed scholarship: See scholarship.

C.N.A.A.: See Council for National Academic Awards.

co-education: Education of boys and girls in the same school or classes.

college: Corporate body which may or may not be part of a university (q.v.) (see also technical college, polytechnic, college of further education, college of education, college of technology, theological college, and college of advanced technology).

college of advanced technology (C.A.T.): College of technology which concentrated entirely on work at undergraduate, postgraduate, and research levels. Since 1965 all ten C.A.T.s have become universities or university colleges.

college of education: College (formerly called a teacher training college) for the training of teachers.

college of further education: College, roughly comparable with a local technical college (q.v.), offering part time and evening courses leading to G.C.E. or technical qualifications or in leisure pursuits.

college of technology: See technical college.

college-based student: Student doing a 'sandwich' course (q.v.) who is enrolled by a college and placed by it in industry for his periods of practical work.

collegiate university: University, like Oxford or London, made up of constituent colleges.

Common Entrance Examination: Selection examination organized on behalf of many of the public schools to determine suitability for admission to such schools at about the age of 13.

commoner: Student of Oxford or Cambridge who has not won a college scholarship (q.v.) or exhibition (q.v.) (though he may hold a scholarship from his local authority).

comprehensive school: Secondary school (q.v.) which takes all the children from a particular area and offers all kinds of courses.

controlled school: Voluntary school (q.v.) for which the local education authority is financially responsible and appoints most of the teachers, but in which the governors or managers have the right to appoint a limited number of teachers who will give special religious instruction. Nearly all controlled schools are C. of E.

Council for National Academic Awards (C.N.A.A.): Successor to the National Council for Technological Awards, awarding first and higher degrees to students in non-autonomous institutions of higher education, like technical colleges.

GLOSSARY

county award: Award to a student by the local education authority. May be a scholarship (q.v.), exhibition (q.v.), or bursary (q.v.).

county college: Institution envisaged in the 1944 Education Act (though none is yet built) to give mainly non-vocational education (q.v.) one day a week to boys and girls between 15 and 18 who have left school.

county organizer: Officer of a local education authority responsible for promoting a particular subject (e.g. drama or physical education) in the authority's schools.

county school: School which is built, maintained, and staffed by the local education authority (q.v.). Its full cost falls on public funds.

crèche: Day nursery (q.v.).

critical period: Stage in a child's development when he is especially susceptible to particular environmental or other influences.

curriculum: Plan of lessons and subjects for a class (q.v.) or school (q.v.).

Dalton plan: Way of arranging school work so that pupils can spend much time in private study.

day continuation school: Institution giving continued education for young workers released for that purpose by their employers.

day nursery: Place where babies and young children may be left while their parents are at work. Not to be confused with a nursery school (q.v.), a day nursery is supervised by the health authority, not the education authority.

day-release: System whereby employers allow days, or parts of days, off for education without loss of pay.

day-school: School whose pupils attend only during working hours and return home every evening.

degree: Qualification given by a university or the C.N.A.A. (q.v.). The bachelor's, or first, degree (e.g. B.A.) can be of two kinds: an honours degree and an ordinary or pass degree. The former is usually of a higher and more specialized standard than the latter and there are normally several classes (q.v.) according to merit. Higher degrees (e.g. M.A., Ph.D.) are awarded after further study or research.

Department of Education and Science (D.E.S.): Government department responsible for education in England and Wales and for universities in Great Britain. (Originally the Board of Education, until 1944, and the Ministry of Education, 1944 to 1964.)

deprived: Expression for a child who lacks something essential for his development, like a home background or mother love.

deputy headmaster (*headmistress, head teacher*): Assistant master (q.v.), of a school appointed as next in status to head teacher.

diploma in technology: Award given by the former National Council for

GLOSSARY

Technological Awards comparable with a university honours degree (q.v.). See C.N.A.A.

direct grant school: Independent school (q.v.) receiving a grant direct from the Ministry of Education subject to special conditions, notably that 25 per cent of the places each year shall be offered, either directly or through the local education authority, to pupils who have at any time previously attended a state school for not less than two years. Half the places may be available for fee-payers.

direct method: Way of teaching languages by concentrating on using them in conversation rather than on formal grammar.

divisional executive for education: Body to whom a local education authority has delegated some of its functions so as to use local knowledge and initiative. Divisional executives for boroughs of over 60,000 people are called excepted districts – excepted because they framed their own schemes of divisional administration.

don: Comprehensive expression for any senior member (teacher) of a university or college, e.g. a fellow (q.v.) or tutor (q.v.).

Education Act, 1944: Principal Act which regulates the present state system of education and provides for the inspection of independent schools.

education committee: Committee composed of members of the local education authority (q.v.) and co-opted experts to which all educational matters are referred, usually for decision and report, but sometimes for recommendation in major questions of policy.

education welfare officer: Originally a school attendance officer, whose main duty was to help to ensure school attendance, he is now much more engaged with the welfare problems of schoolchildren.

educational psychologist: Man or woman who studies human behaviour and the human mind in order to deal with the problems of children and sometimes their teachers.

educational priority areas (E.P.A.s): Areas which the Plowden Report said should be designated by the Secretary of State as in need of special provision because they were educationally and socially deprived.

educationally subnormal (E.S.N.): Expression to describe children whose I.Q. (q.v.) is between about fifty and about eighty, and who therefore require special educational treatment, either in ordinary or in special (E.S.N.) schools.

efficient: See recognized as efficient.

eleven+ examination: Device, which varies from one local authority to another, for selecting children for the secondary schools available.

GLOSSARY

May include any or all of the following: reports from primary school head teachers, intelligence tests (q.v.), tests in English and arithmetic, interviews, statements of parental choice.

evening institute: Establishment for further education (q.v.) having no day-time session and perhaps housed in premises used during the day as ordinary day school.

examinations: See under individual types, e.g. eleven+, group, internal, etc.

exhibition: Award similar to a scholarship (q.v.).

external examination: Examination set by some body outside the school or college attended by the candidates.

extra-mural department (usually of a university): Department which organizes courses for those who are not members of the parent organization.

family grouping (*vertical classification*): Form of grouping children, mainly in infant schools, in which a class includes children of two or three age-groups, e.g. five- to seven-year-olds.

federal university: University formally made up of colleges and other bodies.

fellow: Senior member of a college or learned society.

first degree: see degree.

form: 1) Another name for a class (e.g. form 5b). 2) Another name for an age-group (e.g. fifth form).

form entry: Method of describing the size of a school by the number of forms (or classes) admitted each year. Thus a two-form entry school may have sixty to eighty new pupils each year divided into two forms.

free activity period: Part of school day in which children are encouraged to decide for themselves what they will do.

free periods: 1) Time in a school curriculum for private or unsupervised study. 2) Time when a teacher is not allocated to a class.

Froebel method: System of education pioneered by Froebel emphasizing educational play for young children.

further education: Education (full-time or part-time) after leaving school for young people and adults.

General Certificate of Education (*G.C.E.*): Certificate awarded on the results of external examinations (q.v.) set by nine examining bodies in England and Wales. Most candidates are pupils at secondary schools. It has two levels: 1) ordinary (O) level is normally taken at 16 after a five-year course. 2) Advanced (A) level is normally taken two years after O level at the end of a sixth-form course (q.v.). Candidates for

GLOSSARY

A level may also take 'scholarship' papers in their chosen subjects: these papers are designed to test more than simply factual knowledge. Specified passes at O and A level exempt holders from entrance examinations to universities and professional bodies.

general science: School subject which covers usually physics, chemistry, and biology.

Girls' Public Day School Trust (G.P.D.S.T.): Trust set up to give secondary education for girls. Has some two dozen schools.

governors, board of: Body to whom the head teacher of a school is responsible. In independent schools they are self-appointing or are appointed by the terms of a trust deed. In state schools they are appointed by the local education authority in accordance with an instrument of government. The members of the governing body of a primary school are called managers (q.v.).

graduate: Person who has a university degree (q.v.).

grammar school: Secondary school for more 'academic' pupils who are usually selected after an eleven+ examination (q.v.).

group examination: Examination in which a given number of subjects are compulsory and have to be passed at the same time.

hall of residence: Large house or block to accommodate students at a university (q.v.) or college (q.v.).

head boy (head girl): Leader of a school's prefects (q.v.).

head of department: Person in a school or university responsible for organizing the teaching of a particular subject.

headmaster (headmistress, head teacher): Person in charge of an individual school, responsible to the governors or managers (q.v.), and in state schools to the local education authority.

Headmasters' Conference (H.M.C.): Body of headmasters of boys' public schools (q.v.) who themselves elect new members on the basis of the size of schools and their sixth forms, their academic achievement and their amount of independence.

helper: See ancillary.

Her Majesty's inspector (H.M.I.): Official attached to the Department of Education who inspects state and independent schools and makes reports. There are about 550 H.M.I.s in England and Wales.

high school: Loose term for a secondary school, usually a grammar school (in the U.S.A. a high school is a secondary school).

higher education: Education beyond G.C.E. A level at a university (q.v.), college of technology (q.v.), or college of education (q.v.).

Higher National Certificate, Diploma: See national certificate, diploma.

honours degree: See degree.

GLOSSARY

Incorporated Association of Preparatory Schools (I.A.P.S.): Association of preparatory schools (q.v.) which are recognized as efficient (q.v.) by the Department of Education.

independent school: School outside the state system run solely by its own proprietor or governing body (but see direct grant school).

infant school: Primary school for children from about 5 to 7 or 8.

Initial Teaching Alphabet (I.T.A.): Alphabet invented to help children more quickly over the first stages of learning to read.

Inner London Education Authority (I.L.E.A.): Committee of the Greater London Council which is the education authority for the old London County Council area.

inspector: See Her Majesty's inspector.

intelligence: There is no generally acceptable short definition: mental ability; mental efficiency; the quality measured by intelligence tests.

intelligence quotient (I.Q.): Percentage that the mental age (q.v.) is of the chronological age (e.g. a child of 8 with a mental age of 10 will have an I.Q. of $\frac{10}{8} \times 100$, which is 125). The results of tests of intelligence and general ability are usually expressed as an I.Q.

intelligence test: Test designed to assess intelligence and general ability.

internal examination: Examination set by the school or college attended by the candidates.

junior schools: 1) Primary school for children from about 8 to 11. 2) Department of an independent school taking children under about 13.

late developer: Term used to describe a child whose mental capacity matures notably later than that of most children. Often used of a pupil who shows more evidence of ability than was apparent at 11+.

lecturer: 1) Anyone who lectures or delivers a talk to a group. 2) Member of the staff of a university or college.

Leicestershire experiment: Method of organizing secondary education tried by Leicestershire in which all children went to the same secondary schools at 11+ and could then choose whether to go to grammar schools at 13+. Acceptable as an interim stage only towards secondary reorganization.

liberal studies: Subjects designed to broaden the general education of pupils specializing (q.v.) in science or technical subjects.

Local Education Authority (L.E.A.): County, county-borough or outer London borough council so called because it is responsible for education in its area (see education committee).

GLOSSARY

lower school: Usually the first and second forms of a school (a grammar school (q.v.) expression).

main school: All the forms in a grammar school (q.v.) other than the sixth form (q.v.).

maintained school: School maintained by a local education authority, including county (q.v.), voluntary aided (q.v.), voluntary controlled (q.v.), and special-agreement (q.v.) schools. Called state school in this book.

major works: Building projects costing more than £20,000.

maladjustment: Expression for the state of a child who is emotionally disturbed.

managers: People who compose the governing body of a state primary school (see 'governors'). Appointed by the local education authority in accordance with an instrument of management. In a voluntary school (q.v.) some of the managers are appointed by the voluntary body responsible.

matriculation: Minimum entrance requirement of universities.

means test: Scale by which a parent's income is measured for the purpose of making a grant.

mental age: The age at which the average child can pass the tests that a particular child passes is the latter's mental age (e.g. a child of 5 who is able to pass tests as well as the average child of 10 is said to have a mental age of 10).

middle school: 1) A school for children aged 8 or 9 to 12 or 13. 2) Usually the third and fourth forms of a school (a grammar school (q.v.) expression).

minor works: Building projects costing less than £20,000.

'mock' G.C.E.: An internal examination (q.v.) run by some schools as a rehearsal for the normal G.C.E. examinations (q.v.)

monitor: 1) Pupil, usually in an individual class, who is made responsible for a particular job (e.g. milk monitor, attendance monitor). 2) Similar to a prefect (q.v.) in some schools.

Montessori method: System of education pioneered by Maria Montessori, laying special emphasis on freedom, self-education, and sense and muscle training.

multilateral school: Secondary school which provides grammar, technical, and secondary modern education in separately organized divisions.

national certificate: Technical certificate awarded by a joint committee of the Department of Education and the appropriate professional body (e.g. Institution of Mechanical Engineers). There are two levels of examination: Ordinary (O.N.C.), awarded after three years' part time study and concurrent employment at, say, 19 and roughly comparable with G.C.E. A level (q.v.) and Higher (H.N.C.) awarded after a further two years' part time study and roughly comparable with an ordinary degree (q.v.).

national college: See technical college.

National Council for Technological Awards: Body which awarded the diploma in Technology (q.v.) and membership of the College of Technologists. Now the C.N.A.A. (q.v.).

national diploma: Similar to national certificate (q.v.) – there are ordinary and higher grades, O.N.D. and H.N.D. – but awarded after two or three years' full time study.

non-vocational study: Education not directed towards a job or career.

nursery class: class in a primary school for children under five.

nursery school: School for children under 5.

old boy (old girl): A former pupil of a school.

open scholarship: See scholarship.

Ordinary National Certificate, Diploma: see national certificate, diploma.

organizer: See county organizer.

out-of-school activity: Pursuit which takes place in a school outside formal lessons (e.g. debating or dramatics).

oversize class: No primary school class should contain more than forty pupils and no secondary class more than thirty, according to the Schools Regulations: the classes that do contain more than these numbers are oversize.

Oxbridge: Omnibus word for the universities of Oxford and Cambridge.

paediatrician: Person who specializes in the study of children.

paediatrics: Study of children.

parent-teacher association: Voluntary association of the parents and teachers of a school.

Part III (of the Education Act, 1944): The section of the Act which deals with the registration and inspection of independent schools.

pass degree: See degree.

physical education (P.E.): Current term for what most parents remember as 'gym' or P.T.

play way: Method of educating young children through guided educational play.

GLOSSARY

polytechnic: College or group of colleges designated after 1966 to be a comprehensive institution of higher education and in which advanced courses (q.v.) were to be concentrated.

postgraduate: After a university first degree (q.v.) – an expression used either of a student or of his studies.

prefect: Pupil (usually an older pupil) who has some responsibility for discipline in a school.

preparatory school: Independent school for children between 8 and 13 which normally prepares pupils for public schools (q.v.).

pre-preparatory school: Independent school for children under about 8.

pre-school playgroup: Voluntary part time playgroups, often run by mothers, for children under five.

previous examination: The minimum entrance requirement at Cambridge.

primary school: School for children under 12.

private school: Independent school which is privately owned and not a public school (q.v.).

progressive school: Name applied to an independent school, often co-educational, with comparatively free discipline or a certain amount of self-government by the pupils.

project: Study undertaken by a class (or on occasions even by a whole school) on one broad subject (say, the neighbourhood) through which the normal school subjects are studied.

provincial university: Slightly pejorative expression for a university in England and Wales outside London, except Oxford and Cambridge.

psychiatrist: Qualified doctor who specializes in the treatment of disorders of the mind. A child psychiatrist is one who further specializes in treating children.

psychiatry: Medical treatment of disorders of behaviour and disorders of the mind.

psycho-analyst: Psychiatrist who has specialized in one form of treatment – psychotherapy (q.v.) – and who accepts the teachings of Sigmund Freud or one of his disciples.

psychologist: Man or woman concerned with the scientific study of human behaviour. See also educational psychologist.

psychology: Science of human behaviour and the human mind.

psychotherapy: Persistent exploration of a patient's mental processes in order to help him towards better social and personal adjustment.

public school: Independent, direct grant, or other secondary school controlled by a governing body created by some statute, scheme, or trust deed (c.f. private school).

pupil-teacher ratio: Average number of pupils to a teacher in a school.

GLOSSARY

qualified teacher: Teacher who has successfully taken a course at a training college or university department of education, has been awarded the Teacher's Certificate, and granted qualified teacher status by the Department of Education. A graduate can at present be granted this status without training.

quota system: System designed to distribute teachers fairly among local education authorities. Each is assigned a total of full-time teachers which it is expected not to exceed.

read: 1) To recognize and understand written words and sentences. 2) To study a subject at university.

reading age: The age at which the average child can read as well as a particular child can is the latter's reading age (e.g. a child of 4 who reads as well as the average child of 6 has a reading age of 6).

recognized as efficient (*by the Department of Education*)*:* All independent schools must be registered with the Department of Education, which lays down minimum standards, but they can apply to be recognized as efficient also: this is a much more strenuous test, and recognition gives the school the positive mark of the Department's approval.

redbrick universities: Pejorative term used to describe universities in England and Wales other than Cambridge, Durham, London, Oxford, and some of the new universities.

registered: see recognized as efficient.

religious instruction (*R.I.*)*:* The only subject which state schools are obliged to teach by law: in county (q.v.) and voluntary controlled schools (q.v.) it is given in accordance with an 'agreed syllabus' (q.v.) and parents may withdraw their children from it if they wish. In voluntary aided schools (q.v.) it is under the control of the managers (q.v.) or governors (q.v.). Also called Religious Education (R.E.).

remedial class: Class (usually quite small) for children who are backward (q.v.) in some way or who need special help.

responsions: Minimum entrance requirement for Oxford.

retarded: Backward (q.v.).

'sandwich' course: Advanced course involving alternate periods (usually of six months) of theoretical training in a technical college and of practical training in industry.

scholarship: 1) Name sometimes still given to the 11+ examination (q.v.). 2) Award – of money – given to a student either from public or from private funds. A 'closed' scholarship is one which is confined to stated groups of people (e.g. the sons of clergymen or the children

GLOSSARY

of a particular area). An 'open' scholarship may be entered for by anyone.

school: 1) Building in which children are taught. 2) The people (teachers and pupils) who use a particular school building. 3) See under different types (e.g. primary, grammar, voluntary). 4) Subject to be studied for a degree (q.v.) at university (q.v.) – e.g. the honours school of modern history (see 'read').

school-leaving age: Age at which compulsory education ends. At present it is the leaving date (Easter or Summer) after a pupil's fifteenth birthday. After 1972 it will be after the sixteenth birthday.

Schools Council for the Curriculum and Examinations: Body established in 1964 by the local education authorities and teachers' associations and the Department of Education and Science for research and development in the curriculum and examinations.

secondary modern shool: One of the largest group of secondary schools, offering a general education to children who have not been selected for another type of school after an 11+ examination (q.v.).

secondary school: School for children aged 11 and over.

selective school: School for which the pupils have been selected (usually at 11+) on the grounds that they can benefit from a more 'academic' education. See grammar and technical schools.

senior master (mistress, teacher): Teacher ranking next to deputy headmaster (q.v.), or, where there is no deputy, to the head (q.v.).

setting: Division of an age-group which is already divided into forms (q.v.), into different 'sets' according to ability for some subjects (e.g. a boy in the fourth year may be in form 4b, the top set for mathematics and the bottom set for French).

sixth form: Upper part of a grammar or technical school entered usually after taking G.C.E. O level (q.v.) at 16.

social sciences: Economics, politics, sociology, psychology, anthropology, and the like.

special-agreement school: Voluntary school (q.v.) similar to an aided school (q.v.).

special school: Primary or secondary school for pupils who need special treatment because of some mental or physical handicap or some maladjustment.

special (E.S.N.) school: Special school for educationally subnormal (q.v.) children.

specialist teacher: Teacher who teaches almost exclusively in one subject for which he is qualified.

specialization: Concentration at school or university on one or a few subjects, usually to the exclusion of others.

GLOSSARY

speech therapy: Correction of defects of speech which have physical causes.

state school: School run by a local education authority; the Department of Education does not run schools directly. (See maintained school.)

streaming: Grouping of children in an age-group according to their ability: the A stream has the brightest children, and so on.

student: Pupil at a university or college.

student-teacher: Teacher in training (who usually does teaching practice in a school).

subject examination: Examination, like the G.C.E. (q.v.) in which a candidate may be examined in one or more subjects of his choice.

'swing', the: Jargon for a former tendency among sixth-form pupils to specialize in science rather than arts (q.v.) subjects. It is now (in 1969) swinging back and towards the social sciences.

syllabus: Course of study in a particular subject.

teacher training college: See college of education.

team teaching: Method of school organization developed in the U.S.A. in which teams of teachers take responsibility for large numbers (say, 200) of children – instead of the normal one teacher, one class.

technical college: College of further education offering professional and vocational education and a wide variety of other courses. There are several kinds: a) local college, offering mainly part-time courses for more elementary qualifications, e.g. Ordinary National Certificate (q.v.) and City and Guilds (q.v.); b) area college, offering full-time and part-time courses at a somewhat higher level, e.g. leading to Higher National Certificate (q.v.) and Higher National Diploma (q.v.); c) regional college offering more advanced work including full-time and 'sandwich' courses (q.v.); d) national college offering advanced courses for the work of specialized industries; e) polytechnic (q.v.).

technical school: Secondary school offering an education particularly related to industry, commerce, or agriculture whose pupils are selected after an 11+ examination (q.v.) or at 13.

technician: Man or woman qualified by specialist technical education and practical training to work under a technologist (q.v.).

technologist: Qualified engineer or applied scientist with the degree (q.v.) or comparable qualification and experience in industry required for membership of a professional institution.

term: The academic year is divided into three parts (or terms) separated by holidays or vacations (q.v.). There is talk of a four-term year.

GLOSSARY

theological college: College for training priests or clergymen.

time-table: Plan of lessons and activities in a school.

training college: See college of education.

'trend', the: Jargon for the increasing tendency of pupils to stay at school beyond the compulsory school-leaving age (q.v.).

tripartite system: Theoretical division of secondary education into grammar, technical, and secondary modern schools: secondary education is in practice 'bipartite' (q.v.).

tripos: Final examination at Cambridge, normally in two parts, the first of which is taken at the end of a student's first or second year, the second at the end of his third.

tutor: 1) Teacher of a single pupil rather than a class. 2) A member of a college staff with particular responsibility, moral or academic, for some students.

tutorial system: A system of teaching in which a student has some tuition on his own, or in a very small group of students, with a tutor.

undergraduate: Student reading for a first degree at a university.

union: 1) Students' union at a university or college. This is primarily a social club consisting often of various sporting and other clubs and societies, but it can also be a means of expressing students' views on university policy towards them. 2) There is a National Union of Students and a number of teachers' unions of which by far the largest and most representative is the National Union of Teachers. 3) In Oxford and Cambridge, and to some extent in some other universities, the union society is the undergraduate debating society.

university: Chartered institution taking pupils over about 18, devoted to advanced study and research, which has the right to grant the qualification of a degree (q.v.).

university department of education: Institution for training graduates (q.v.) as teachers.

University Grants Committee: Body which distributes Government grants of money to individual universities.

upper school: 1) Usually fifth and sixth forms of a school. A grammar school (q.v.) expression. 2) Secondary part of an independent or direct grant school.

urban programme: interdepartmental attempt to aid deprived urban areas with additional building programmes and grants. Education's share is chiefly for nursery schools.

vacation: Period between university terms: not called a holiday, because, in theory at least, students and staff spend a large part of the time continuing their work.

GLOSSARY

vertical classification: See family grouping.

village college: A secondary modern school and a community centre designed as one: the best-known examples are in Cambridgeshire.

visual aids: Pictures, charts, models, filmstrips, films, and television used by teachers in their lessons.

vocational education: Education or training primarily for a career or job.

voluntary school: School built by a voluntary body (e.g. a denomination) but maintained by the local education authority. (See aided, controlled, and special agreement schools.)

work-based student: Student doing a 'sandwich' (q.v.) course who is the employee of a particular firm.

year: Way of referring to groups in a school by age (e.g. the 'first year' of a grammar school would be the pupils who have just arrived).

youth employment service: Service usually locally organized by the local education authority but directed and controlled (and in some areas locally organized) by the Ministry of Labour, dealing with the employment and careers of young people from 15 to 18.

youth service: Provision of recreational facilities for young people by the Department of Education, local authorities, and voluntary bodies.

Index

accommodation, school, 42–3, 53
administrative memoranda, 43
Admission to Grammar Schools, 120
adult education, 33, 183–4
advancement of state education, association for the, 16, 196
advisers, county, 58, 70
Advisory Centre for Education, 13, 103, 196
agreed syllabus, 77
aided schools, 78–9, 109
Albemarle Committee, 50, 184
Alfred the Great, 93
all-age schools, 75, 76, 86, 94
Anderson, Sir Colin, 50
Andrew, Sir Herbert, 31
Anglesey, 90
apprenticeship, 177–9
approved schools, 41
arbitration, 71
art education, 33, 58, 176, 184
articles of government and management, 78
Arts Council, 34
Associated Examining Board, 128, 130
Association of Headmistresses, 110, 196
Association of Municipal Corporations, 71

Baker, Mrs Joy, 147
bilateral schools, 94, 97
Board of Education, 17, 47, 86, 178
Board of Education, President of the, 17, 26, 108
Board of Management for Common Entrance, 122
Board of Trade, 26
boarding, 41, 54, 55, 73, 103–7, 110, 112, 148, 150, 152, 154, 160, 163–9
Borstal institutions, 41
Boyle, Sir Edward, 29, 49
Bristol, 90
British Broadcasting Corporation, 185
building, programmes for school, 38–40
building standards, 39, 53, 157
Burnham Committee, 21, 70–72
Butler, R. A., 17, 18, 26, 108

Cabinet, the 26, 28–9
Central Advisory Councils for Education, 24, 47–50
central schools, 94, 97
Central Training Council, 180–81
Certificate of Secondary Education, 49, 93, 135–9
Chancellor of the Exchequer, 28, 113, 191
chief education officer, 54, 63, 120 143
child employment, 55
Church of England schools, 74–7
circulars, 43, 81
City and Guilds, examinations of, 175, 177, 181
civic universities, 188–9

INDEX

Clarendon Commission on the public schools, 108–9
classes, in schools, 66–7, 172 (*and see* size of classes)
cleansing, 158
clothing, 55
co-education, 63, 80, 83, 92, 94, 95, 102, 106, 110, 112, 141, 150, 153, 160–62
colleges of advanced technology, 58, 176, 179, 189–90, 193
colleges of art, 58, 174
colleges of education, 22, 54, 68–70, 174, 184–5, 193
commerce, colleges of, 175
Common Entrance Examination for public schools, 107, 414, 121–8
comprehensive schools, 43, 48, 61, 62, 65, 75, 86, 89–91, 95–6, 112
Comptroller-General, 191
compulsory education, 20, 54, 59–60, 62, 80
Conservative Party, 91
controlled schools, 74–7, 78, 109
Council for Educational Advance, 17
Council for National Academic Awards, 179–80, 194
Council for Scientific Policy, 33
councillors, 57, 63, 143
councils, county and county borough, 20, 52, 55–7 (*and see* local education authorities)
county colleges, 21, 47–8, 54, 183
County Councils Association, 71
county schools, 54–5, 74 (*and see* state schools)
courts, the, 60–61, 146

Coventry, 90
craft courses, 177–8, 181
Crosland, Anthony, 26
Crowther Report, 47–8, 89
Croydon plan, 90

day nurseries, 81
degrees, 191, 192
  education, 185, 193
  first, 191–2
  higher, 192–3
denominational schools, 18, 19, 20, 21, 74–8, 79, 86, 141, 143
dental services and inspections, 158–9
Department of Education and Science, 11, 13, 23, 24–51, 59–9, 65, 68, 71–2, 75, 78, 87, 89, 100, 102–5, 141–2, 175, 178, 180, 184, 191, and *passim* (*and see* Ministry of Education)
  annual report of, 24
  branches of, 31–4
development group, in Department of Education's architects and building branch, 40
Devonshire, 90
diploma in technology, 176, 179
direct grant schools, 65, 99, 101–3, 109–10, 155, 158, 176,
discipline, 152, 167

Eccles, Sir David (now Lord), 26
Ede, J. Chuter, 17, 18
Education Act, 1944, 16, 17, 20–28, 40–42, 47, 51–3, 56, 59, 61–3, 70, 76–7, 78, 83, 85–7 103, 116, 140, 143–7, 157, 173–4, 182–3

222

INDEX

education acts, 1936, 19
  1946, 1948, 1953, 22
  1962, 22, 60
  1963 (Remuneration of Teachers Act), 22, 71
  1964, 22, 65, 85
  1965 (Remuneration of Teachers Act), 71
  1967, 22
  1968, 22–3
education bills, 30, 36
education committees, 56–8, 63, 143, (*and see* local education authorities)
educationally subnormal (E.S.N.), 98–100
elections, 56–7, 63, 89–90
elementary education, and schools, 19, 32, 52–3, 92–3, 97
eleven plus examination, and procedures, 85, 88–9, 91, 101, 106, 114, 115–21, 152, 155, 171
Enfield Borough Council, 61, 91
entry qualifications, colleges of advanced technology, 176
  training colleges, 69
  universities, 134–5, 186
equal opportunity, 89
equal pay, 21
Essex County Council, 57
evening institutes, 183
examining boards, for the General Certificate of Education, 128
excepted districts, 52
Exchequer, 42, 72, 190–91

family grouping, 172
farm institutes, 58, 70, 176
federal universities, 187–9
fees (*see* school fees)

finance, 11, 37–8, 56, 190, 198–203
Finance Act, 1968, 113, 156
Fleming Committee, 108
forms, in schools, 66–7
full-time education, compulsory, 61–2 (*and see* compulsory education)
further education, 11, 20, 21, 44, 52, 54, 71, 173–84

General Certificate of Education, 51, 69, 88, 93–4, 97, 103–4, 111, 114–15, 128–36, 173–5, 191
general grants, 37–8, 42, 199–203
Girls' Public Day School Trust, 102
Girls' School Year Book, 110
Godfrey Thomas Unit for Educational Research (Edinburgh University), 117
Governing Bodies Association, 108–9, 112
Governing Bodies of Girls' Public Schools Association, 112
governors, of schools, 22, 40, 53, 64, 74–5, 77–90, 101–2
graduates as teachers, 49, 68–9, 72, 83, 97, 102, 107, 184
grammar schools 18, 61–3, 65, 88–90, 93–4, 95–6, 102, 109–10, 111, 113–14, 123–4, 140, 155, 171
Greater London Council, 52, 55

handicapped children, 21, 32, 53, 58, 98–101 (*and see* special education)
Handicapped Pupils and Special Schools Regulations, 1959, 98

INDEX

head teachers, 12, 63–4, 72–3, 78–80, 83, 102, 107, 140, 150
Headmasters' Conference, 102–3, 108–9, 112, 121–2
higher education, 173–84, 192–4 (*and see* various kinds of higher education)
Higher School Leaving Certificate, 87
Hogg, Quintin, 25
holidays, 62, 79
Home Office, 41
homosexuality, 152, 162, 166, 169
Horsbrugh, Lady, 26
houses, and housemasters, 67–8

immigrant children, 32
Incorporated Association of Preparatory Schools, 108, 122
independent schools, 11, 12, 40, 55, 65, 72, 82, 103–13, 114, 148–56, 158
  recognition as efficient, 41, 104
  registration, 21, 40–41, 65, 103
  tribunal, 41
Industrial Training Act, 1964, 32, 48, 177, 180–82
infant schools, 63–4, 65, 75, 83–5, 114, 172 (*and see* primary schools)
Inner London Education Authority, 52, 56, 71
inspections, medical and dental, 158–9
inspectors, Her Majesty's, 44–7, 70, 104, 148–9
  local authority, 55, 71
  reports, 44–7
institutes of education, 184
instruments of management and government, 77–8

instruments, statutory, 42
intelligence tests, 88–9, 115

James Report, 194
junior schools, 58, 64, 65, 75–6, 83, 85–6, 114 (*and see* primary schools)
junior with infant schools, 65, 75, 83–4 (*and see* primary schools)
junior without infant schools, 75, 83 (*and see* primary schools)

Labour Party, 28, 89, 113, 185
Law, the, 60–64, 147
Leicestershire plan, 90
leisure-time activities, 21, 54
local authority associations, 38, 71, 196
Local Authority Practices in the Allocation of Pupils to Secondary Schools, 120
local education authorities, 12, 20, 21, 25–8, 51–9, 62–4, 70–75, 78–82, 98, 100–102, 116–17, 120–21, 128, 139–45, 151, 154–5, 183–4, 190, 197, 198–203
  duties, 54–5
  officers, 58, 198
  powers, 54–5
local health authorities, 98, 100
London boroughs, 52, 55
London County Council, 52, 71, 90 (*and see* Greater London Council)

Macmillan, Harold, 31
maintained schools, 12, 54–5, 73, 99, 112 (*and see* state schools)
maintenance grants, 21, 22, 50, 154 (*and see* student grants)

INDEX

major (building) works, 39
maladjusted children, 58, 99–100
managers, of schools, 40, 53–5, 74, 77–90
manpower, highly qualified, advisory committee on, 33
Manual of Guidance, Schools No. 1, 43, 141, 142
married women, 70
meals and milk, school, 21, 32, 55, 154, 157–8
medical inspections, and services, 21, 32, 54, 157–9
Members of Parliament, 24–5, 143, 147
Membership of the College of Technologists, 179
Metropolitan Regional Examinations Board, 137
middle schools, 65, 85–6
Middlesex County Council, 57
Minister for Science, 26
Minister of Education, 20, 23, 25–8, 71, 81, 87, 98 (*and see* Secretary of State for Education and Science)
Minister of Labour, 180
Minister of State, 31
ministerial policy, 28–9, 34, 43–4
Minister of Education, 23, 50, 95, 184 (*and see* Department of Education and Science)
Ministry of Housing and Local Government, 37
Ministry of Labour, 180–81
Ministry of Technology, 26
minor (building) works, 39
'Moray House' tests, 117
multilateral schools, 94, 97
municipal boroughs, 53
museums, 41
music education, 33, 58

National Advisory Council for Education in Industry and Commerce, 50
National Advisory Council on the Training and Supply of Teachers, 50
National Association of Schoolmasters, 71
national certificates and diplomas, 97, 175, 177–9
National Council for Technological Awards, 179
National Foundation for Educational Research, 115, 120
National Health Service, 158
National Nursery Examination Board, 82
National Union of Teachers, 25, 71, 157, 196
N.A.T.O., 33
Newsom Report, 47–9
Newsom, Sir John, 111
Norfolk, 147
Northern Ireland, 11
Nuffield Foundation, 51
nursery education, and schools, 32, 49, 53, 58, 65, 80–84, 105, 114, 169–70

O.E.C.D., 33
Open University, 33, 185–6
operatives, 177–8
organizers, county, 58, 70
out-of-school activities, 73, 94, 96, 152

parents, 11–12, 15–16, 34
parents' associations, 16, 196
 choice, 13, 43, 122–3, 140–56
 duties, 16, 98, 144–5
 rights, 54, 58–63, 77, 139–47

225

INDEX

Parliament, 16, 24–5, 30–31, 57, 60–62, 65, 190–91
Parliamentary counsel, 36
Parliamentary Private Secretary, 31
Parliamentary Secretary, 30–31
Pelham Committee, 70
Pidgeon, D. A., 120
Plan for Polytechnics and Other Colleges, A, 176
play-groups, 82, 196
playing-fields, 43
Plowden Report, 47, 49, 86
polytechnics, 43, 174, 176–7
prefects, 68, 73
preparatory schools, 65, 105–8, 114–15, 122
pre-preparatory schools, 65, 105–6
Pre-School Play-groups Association, 82, 196
primary education, and schools, 20, 43, 45, 49, 52–3, 58, 63, 65, 70, 73, 75, 76, 81, 83–6, 100–101, 105–8, 114–15, 120, 124, 151, 157–8
Principles of Government in Maintained Secondary Schools (White Paper), 78
Private Office, 35
Procedures for the Allocation of Pupils in Secondary Education, 120
professional bodies, 44, 129, 179
progressive schools, 108, 111, 148
Public and Preparatory Schools Year Book, 110, 155
Public Libraries and Museums Act, 1964, 33
public schools, 12, 65, 103, 107–15, 121–4, 148–56, 161
Public Schools Commission, 108–9, 111–13
punishment, 152, 167
pupil–teacher ratio, 82–4, 92–3, 95, 99, 102–5, 107

qualified teacher status, 69, 72
quota system, for teachers, 70

rates, 37, 56, 153, 158
recognition as efficient (*see under* independent schools)
Regional Examining Unions, 181
registration (*see under* independent schools)
regulations, statutory, 42–4, 62
religious education, 18, 21, 32, 41, 54, 74–7, 110, 111, 114, 141, 153 (*and see* denominational schools)
research, 33, 55
Robbins Committee, 89, 173–4, 176, 179, 182, 185, 190, 193
Roman Catholic schools, 74–7, 121–2, 141
Royal Society of Arts, examinations of, 97, 175, 177
rules, statutory, 42–4

sandwich courses, 179, 190
school attendance order, 144–7
School Certificate Examination, 129
school dental officer, 58
school fees, 102–3, 105–6, 112–13, 148–51, 153–6
school-leaving age, 19, 20, 21, 27, 47–8, 51, 59–60, 65, 87, 92, 98, 113, 170–71
school-leaving certificate, 87, 94
school-leaving dates, 22, 48, 59–61

INDEX

school medical officer, 58
school starting age, 59, 66, 80, 83, 113
school welfare officer, 59
schools, 11, 63–115 (*and see* under various kinds of schools)
Schools Council for the Curriculum and Examinations, 50–51, 129
Schools Regulations, 1959, 42, 62, 84
Science in Primary Schools (Ministry of Education pamphlet), 46
Scotland, 11
Scottish Education Department, 50
Scottish universities, 187
secondary education; and schools, 18, 20, 32, 44, 49, 52–3, 58, 61–2, 65, 70, 73, 78, 79, 86–7, 92, 94–6, 151, 157, 173
reorganization of, 86–92, 112
secondary modern schools, 61–2, 65, 75, 87–8, 92–3, 110, 114, 135
Secondary School Examinations Council, 50, 51
Secretary of State for Education and Science, 23, 25–30, 35–9, 42, 56, 62–3, 71, 78–9, 81, 89–90, 98, 111, 129, 144–7, 190, 194 (*and see* Minister of Education)
Service Departments, 41
sets, in schools, 66–7
sex education, 53, 161–2
'shadow' Ministers, 24
size of classes, in schools, 42, 48, 82, 84, 92–3, 95, 99–100, 103, 113, 148
size of schools, 83, 92–3, 94–5, 99, 102, 105, 107

special agreement schools, 74–7
special education and schools, 21, 22, 58, 97–101
special services, 21, 32, 34, 54, 157–9
speech day, 79
Spens Report, 95
Standards for School Premises Regulations, 1959, 42
state schools, 12–13, 65, 72, 73–101, 105–6, 110, 113–14, 123–4, 140–47, 148–9, 150–51, 153 (*and see* various kinds of schools)
Stockholm experiment, 89
streaming, 67, 85, 114, 171–2
student grants, 50, 112
syllabuses, 66, 182

taxes, 37, 153, 156
teachers, 11, 45, 55, 59, 63, 68–73, 75, 83, 92–3, 95, 100, 102–5, 107, 114, 121–2, 135, 149–50, 151–2, 160, 161, 163–5, 168, 172
teachers' associations, 25, 44, 50, 71–2, 196–7
pensions, 72
salaries, 22, 70–72
superannuation, 22, 32, 72
training (*see* colleges of education)
Teachers' Superannuation Act, 1967, 22
technical colleges, 22, 32, 58, 174–6, 179–80, 182, 193–4
area, local, national and regional colleges, 175–6
qualifications, 177–80
schools, 18, 75, 94–7
teachers, 71, 184

INDEX

technicians, 177, 181
tests (11 plus), 116–19
traffic dangers, 142
training colleges (*see* colleges of education)
transfer, from primary to secondary school, 49, 65, 85–6, 90–91, 95, 105, 111, 123–4
transport, to school, 54, 60
Treasury, the, 31
'trend', the, 87
tripartite system, 90–91

U.N.E.S.C.O., 33
uniform, school, 106, 154
union of women teachers, 196
universities, 11, 21, 25, 33, 41, 55, 58, 68, 109, 114, 128–9, 134, 174, 176, 179–80, 183–94
Universities Central Council on Admissions, 135
university entrance, 48, 129, 134, 193
  government, 190–91
University Grants Committee, 11, 25, 33, 41, 58, 185, 190–91
University of the Air, 185

urban districts, 52

verminous pupils, 54
vertical classification, 172
vocational education, 32–3, 48, 93, 95, 174, 182–3
voluntary schools, 22, 32, 55, 74–7 (*and see* denominational schools *and* state schools)

Wales, Education Office for, 34
walking distance, to school, 60
welfare services, 21, 32 (*and see* special services)
Welsh Joint Educational Committee, 71
Welsh language, 141
Westmorland, 90
Wordie, J. S., 71
Workers' Educational Association, 183

Yates, A., 120
youth employment bureaux, 58, 180, 184
  officers, 58, 70
youth service, 32, 50, 184

'zoning', 142

MORE ABOUT PENGUINS
AND PELICANS

Penguinews, which appears every month, contains details of all the new books issued by Penguins as they are published. From time to time it is supplemented by *Penguins in Print*, which is a complete list of all available books published by Penguins. (There are well over three thousand of these.)

A specimen copy of *Penguinews* will be sent to you free on request, and you can become a subscriber for the price of the postage. For a year's issues (including the complete lists) please send 30p if you live in the United Kingdom, or 60p if you live elsewhere. Just write to Dept EP, Penguin Books Ltd, Harmondsworth, Middlesex, enclosing a cheque or postal order, and your name will be added to the mailing list.

Note: *Penguinews* and *Penguins in Print* are not available in the U.S.A. or Canada

RISINGHILL

DEATH OF A COMPREHENSIVE SCHOOL

Leila Berg

'Wild school is tamed by love'

'Does sparing the rod breed crime?'

'Parents will fight move to close school'

The school which produced these headlines in 1964 and 1965 was Risinghill, a co-educational comprehensive in Islington.

This is its story, told often in the words of pupils and parents, the story of its courageous headmaster, Michael Duane, and the story of its eventual closure. It is a passionate indictment of educational bureaucracy and bureaucrats, of intolerance and stupidity. It is a story in which the word 'love' occurs again and again, in neither a sentimental nor a titillating way, but as a key word in a basic conflict about the state education of children. It is a sad story, written in anger and without fear.

THE UNIVERSITIES

V. H. H. Green

The universities have always played a vital role in British society, but in the last fifty years their importance has increased as dramatically as their numbers. The resulting changes – and the need to understand them – have been very much in Dr Green's mind in writing this book.

His text provides a much-needed short history of the 'stone' universities – Scottish as well as English – from their medieval foundations to the present day, but he has concentrated equally on the development of the 'red-brick' and 'plate-glass' universities and on the present role of university education as a whole in British society.

By relating the present system to its history and to social conditions Dr Green has shed light both on the present and past relevance of Britain's universities to her overall development.